UNDERST
ALCOH

D0660015

BOOKS IN THE **LIFELINES FOR RECOVERY** SERIES

Zondervan's **Lifelines for Recovery** series emphasizes healthy, step-by-step approaches for dealing with specific critical issues.

UNDERSTANDING
Answers to Questions People Ask
ALCOHOLISM

Carolyn Johnson

ZondervanPublishingHouse
Grand Rapids, Michigan

A Division of HarperCollinsPublishers

UNDERSTANDING ALCOHOLISM
Copyright © 1991 by Carolyn Johnson

Requests for information should be addressed to:
Zondervan Publishing House
1415 Lake Drive, S.E.
Grand Rapids, Michigan 49506

Library of Congress Cataloging-in-Publication Data

Johnson, Carolyn, 1926–
    Understanding alcoholism / Carolyn Johnson.
      p. cm.
    Includes bibliographical references.
    ISBN 0-310-52281-1 (pbk.)
     1. Alcoholism. 2. Alcoholism—Religious aspects—Christianity.
  II. Title.
  HV5060.J55 1991
  362.29′2—dc20
                                                 90–9042
                                                  CIP

Unless otherwise noted, all Scripture quotations are taken from the *Holy Bible: New International Version* (North American Edition), copyright © 1973, 1978, 1984 by the International Bible Society. Used by permission of Zondervan Bible Publishers.

MY CASE HISTORIES ARE COMPOSITES—REAL SITUATIONS OF REAL PEOPLE WITH THE DETAILS CHANGED ENOUGH TO PROTECT THEIR PRIVACY.

Printed in the United States of America

Edited by Nia Jones
Designed by Kim Koning

91 92 93 94 95 96 / AK / 7 6 5 4 3 2 1

This edition is printed on acid-free paper and meets the American National Standards Institute Z39.48 standard.

For my husband Harry,
   who has walked beside me on our recovery road,
   who has endured my failures and celebrated
      my successes,
   whose own life is a testimony of God's
      healing grace.

Contents

Acknowledgments

My thanks to:

The hundreds of anonymous individuals who have been there when I needed them. They shared their experience, strength, and hope with me and saved my life.

My fellow scribes of the Santa Ynez Valley Presbyterian Church Writers' Club and our leader Carol Lacy, who helped me to write what I know. They gave me the courage to finish this book.

My incomparable friend, Barbra Minar, who was always just a phone call away, ready to listen to another paragraph or page. She understood the struggle behind the words.

The women of Valley Bible Fellowship, who were faithful to pray as I wrote. They helped me remain Christ-centered.

My beloved blended family, who gave me permission to tell you about myself.

Introduction

The writing of this book has been like a long pregnancy—conceived in a dark period before I had words to express what was happening to me; nurtured and brought to term by the grace of God; and born to celebrate the miracle of sobriety in my life. Labor began as my experience replayed itself in my memory and as people I love shared their pain with me. At the end there was a struggle against the birth of a finished manuscript, knowing how vulnerable I would be to the condemnation of those who might not understand.

And that's what this book is all about—understanding alcoholism. We who have been trapped by our addiction to this legal and socially acceptable drug yearn for understanding. If there is an alcoholic in your life (and chances are four in ten that there is), you may be tired of trying to understand. But understanding will help you live with your circumstances—or change them. If you are angry, I pray you may find some compassion for your alcoholic, which will lighten your burden of resentment. If you feel guilty, you'll find assurance that you are not responsible for anyone else's drinking; you didn't cause it and can't control it. If you are afraid, I pray you'll find reason to hope and the faith to replace your fear.

I thought for a long time before I decided to identify myself as a recovering alcoholic. Brave people like Betty

Ford have helped me to decide. Anyone who knew me twenty or thirty years ago already has known about my alcoholism. Others in this small town where we have lived for the last three decades have probably heard. To hide behind a pseudonym wouldn't fit with what I believe—that alcoholism is a disease and not a cause for shame.

There are thousands like me who have been released from their bondage to alcohol or other drugs. We are mostly anonymous. You would pass us on the street without recognizing anything different about us. We are free and living normal lives by God's grace. In freeing us, God freed those who loved us and became the innocent victims of our disease. We can testify to God's power to change lives. He can change yours.

We are deeply sorry for the pain we've caused and the lives we've disrupted. Part of our recovery process is reaching out to those who still suffer from addictive illness—to the sick alcoholic or to the family member who reaps the bitter harvest. In answering some of the questions you ask us, we are reaching out to you. I pray that you will find help within these pages.

UNDERSTANDING ALCOHOLISM

"Is It Really a Disease?"

When did it happen that the "town drunk" became just an unfortunate victim of the disease of alcoholism? Those who live with the alcoholic—the wives, sons, sisters, and fathers—protest that *they* are the true victims.

"Isn't it a cop-out," people ask, "calling alcoholism a disease when people bring it on themselves by uncontrolled drinking?" That's a logical question asked by many who see excessive drinking as sin instead of sickness. However, alcoholism fits the definition of disease as given by the American Heritage Dictionary: "An abnormal condition of an organism or part, esp. as a consequence of infection, inherent weakness, or environmental stress, that impairs physiological functioning."

"There you go," they say. "It says 'inherent weakness,' doesn't it?"

"Yes, it does, and it is, but maybe not in the way you're thinking," I answer.

It has taken nearly three decades for me to speak of

17

my own alcoholic affliction as "my disease." The fact that the American Medical Association officially recognized alcoholism as a bona fide illness in 1957 undoubtedly helped many of us along the road to sobriety in the years that followed. Even so, that diagnosis seemed more like a good excuse for bad behavior to many people.

I was a champion excuse-maker. I *wanted* alcoholism to be a disease. I wanted the world to believe that it hadn't been my fault after all, but I couldn't quite believe it myself. I couldn't seem to control my drinking, so secretly I blamed my lack of control on a weakness of character or some personality flaw that affected me alone. Alone, that is, except for the down-and-outers I'd seen on Main Street in Los Angeles or in the Tenderloin District in San Francisco. I'd heard of an occasional "dipsomaniac" in someone's family closet, but never, as my mother would say, among "our kind."

AN UNEXPECTED DEVELOPMENT

As a conservative young homemaker, mother of four little ones, and wife of a professional man, I *should* have been able to drink like others in our circle of friends, to enjoy a relaxing cocktail before dinner, a cold beer on a hot day, or a glass of fine wine with a delicious meal. I didn't break out in a rash when I drank nor did I show any other external symptoms of my allergy to alcohol—not at first, anyway.

In the beginning, all of my reactions to alcohol were internal and wonderful. One drink began a warm glow deep inside, softening the kinks of self-consciousness that seemed to warp my personality. At last I felt connected to other people. Alcohol rounded my square-peg corners so that I suddenly fit into the circle of those around me. This occasional social drinking seemed harmless enough, but it was the key that unlocked the door to addiction.

When my four-year-old son died from a sudden illness, alcohol became a poultice for my throbbing grief. "Come and have a drink," someone said, and I discovered that alcohol had the power to dull pain. A cocktail before dinner became a necessary ritual—one I anticipated like a postoperative patient might await his next injection of morphine. Alcohol helped melt the glacier of tears that weighed upon my heart.

So I found a release from self-consciousness and a relief from pain. I learned to suppress my inexpressible grief and laugh again. Alcohol was my friend—a bridge across dark waters into a land of make-believe happiness.

At the end of my descent into alcoholism, the joy had gone out of me like air from a leaky balloon. Alcohol had become the focal point of my life, the reason for my existence. My days became a frantic search to recapture the exquisite glow I'd experienced when I first drank, but it eluded me. Instead of fitting in with the people around me, now I became isolated in a prison of despair. I could no longer escape or suppress the pain of living.

Glimpses of Reality

There were intervals of relative clarity, a few hours at the beginning of each day, when I had a glimpse of what I was doing to myself and my family and felt heart-wrenching remorse. *I will stop*, I promised myself. *I will stop today*. Or, at least, I wouldn't have a drink before five in the afternoon—or maybe four, if I washed the living room windows and waxed the hardwood floors. What I would do, I'd decided by noon, was to limit myself to a reasonable amount of alcohol. *One glass of wine with my ham sandwich couldn't hurt,* I reasoned to myself. But after all the scrubbing and polishing, the pressures of motherhood, the nagging worry about my deteriorating marriage, the phone call to tell me that I'd missed the dental appointment I couldn't remember making, and the blankety-blank cat that was hanging by his toenails from the screen door—well, there was no way I could get beyond three o'clock without a drink to calm my nerves. *Tomorrow will be a better day. Tomorrow,* I promised myself, *I will do something about my drinking.*

Unfortunately, tomorrow was always one day away. In an occasional flash of self-honesty, I could see that I'd brought this misery on myself. By using and abusing what others managed to enjoy in appropriate ways and on special occasions, I had built a wall that separated me from friends and family. The magic potion that I'd counted on to help me cope with life and people had turned to poison.

Reaching Out

Finally I cried out to an unknown God for help. And then God led me to a group of people who were struggling with the same malady. "We are not bad people trying to be good," my new friends told me. "We are sick people trying to get well."

Maybe, I thought. I wanted to believe them. But I thought that if alcoholism was any kind of a disease, it must be a type of mental illness. I balked at thinking of myself as mentally ill, but the only other choice was that I was "bad," which led to self-blame and self-hatred. The "disease" theory *seemed* like a cop-out, a gimmick, to take away the shame some of us alcoholics felt over our lack of control. My scepticism made for a slow recovery. Guilt weighed upon me like one of those lead aprons an x-ray technician uses, blocking even God's forgiveness.

"But isn't drunkenness a sin?"

As I look around me today with sober eyes and a backlog of hands-on research, I am beginning to understand that what I have now in remission, and had once in its active form, is an illness. I became exposed to it in a world of social drinking, in a society where this most lethal of drugs is approved and accepted.

Alcoholism is a disease by medical definition. That doesn't negate the biblical admonitions about drunkenness. The Bible makes it clear that drunkenness *is* sin. Drunkards are named among thieves, adulterers, and slanderers as those who will not inherit the kingdom of God (1 Cor. 6:9–10). Paul goes on to remind the believer, "And that is what some of you were. But you were washed, you were sanctified, you were justified in the name of the Lord Jesus Christ and by the Spirit of our God" (1 Cor. 6:11). As Christians, we know that we are all sinners saved by grace. Adam's legacy of sin has left us all weak in one way or another. If we think we are not, we suffer from the greatest weakness of all—that of pride. As Paul writes to the Romans:

> For the good that I would, I do not: but the evil which I would not, that I do. Now if I do that I would not, it is no more I that do it, but sin that dwelleth in me. I find then a law, that, when I would do good, evil is present with me.
>
> (Rom. 7:19–21 KJV)

The alcoholic *knows* that his drinking opens the door

to a world of sin. He continually finds himself acting in a way that he abhors and repeatedly vows to change his ways. But he is powerless to keep those vows until he understands the nature of his physical addiction.

Jodi Dittmar, a Christian family counselor, once told me:

> God created us as triune beings. We are body, mind, and spirit, all of one piece. When the body is sick, so is the spirit. I don't attempt to counsel alcoholics until they have gone for treatment of their physical addiction. The mind and spirit cannot function in a healthy manner until the body is healed of its illness.

I was not a Christian in the days when my alcoholism was in its active stage. Had I been, my history might have been different; I'll never know. The God I understood then in a vague sort of way made me very aware of my transgressions. My conscience had not become so callous that it ceased to function, so when I hurt bad enough, I was driven to my knees. God heard my frantic prayers and came running to meet me as I groped my way toward Him. My alcoholism has certainly been a blight upon my life, but it served as the first rung of the ladder I would climb toward the knowledge of Jesus Christ and His saving grace.

Even now, my solid faith does not protect me completely from slipping back into my addiction. In my humanity, I will always be vulnerable. I've learned that I cannot drink alcohol ever again. I learned this lesson in a secular, though spiritual, program to which God led me in my desperate need

"Well, it's not my problem, is it?"

Chances are four in ten that it is or will become your problem. Experts estimate that one in ten people who drink beverage alcohol either are or will become alcoholic. Each of these people will have a life-altering effect on at least three others. If you and the members of your family have escaped the devastating effects of the disease of alcoholism, you are fortunate. Even so, you probably live somewhere within the "fallout zone."

If you drive a car, you could be affected because a frightening percentage of your fellow drivers are alcohol-impaired. On Saturday nights, the party-goers and heavy social drinkers are an expected menace. On a mid-week morning, the drunk driver is likely to be an alcoholic who lost his weekend somewhere in a periodic binge.

My friend Beth left a luncheon at two o'clock on a Thursday afternoon to drive the five miles from our small town to her country home. She and her husband were looking forward to meeting their grown children the next day at a mountain resort for a skiing weekend, and Beth was happily anticipating their reunion when she saw another car speeding toward her in the wrong lane of the narrow road. She was able to swerve out of the direct path of the oncoming car, so she wasn't killed or even badly injured. But the repercussions of that accident included a demolished car, a spoiled weekend, and many months of treatment for wrenched muscles.

The driver of the other car was, and is, an alcoholic. His occasional attempts to stay sober are interspersed with periodic binges. He is not the "town drunk," but a talented and successful man. He is respected by his peers, many of whom are unaware of the severity of his problem with alcohol.

Beth is only one among thousands of innocent victims of *someone else's* alcoholism. The next victim could be you or someone you love.

"What kind of person becomes an alcoholic?"

All kinds of people are alcoholics. Contrary to popular belief, professionals in the field say there are no alcoholic personality "types." The common characteristics displayed by people in treatment are more likely to be a result of their illness rather than the cause. The disease of alcoholism strikes the most unlikely targets—people who have demonstrated maturity, moderation, and strength of character in every other area of their lives. It is no respecter of sex, socioeconomic level, or age group.

Consider the story of a lady I shall call Victoria Corbett. Victoria and I met at a conference, where she happened to confide in me that she was a newly-sober alcoholic.

"I'd never had a drink in my life until I was fifty-four years old," she said. "My family belonged to a denomination that frowned on the use of alcohol, and my husband, Ted, had been raised the same way. Our social life revolved around the church, and even outside the church our particular friends and neighbors didn't drink. Oh, maybe some of them would have an occasional glass of wine at a dinner party, but that was all.

"Ted died suddenly a few years ago. It was a blow, but I managed to adjust with the help of my friends and family. After I got over that intense period of grief, I established a pretty satisfying life for myself, working part-time in a local gift shop, staying active in my church, and visiting my grown children and grandchildren. The only real problem I had was insomnia. I thought perhaps my sleeplessness was caused by menopause, so I went for a check-up.

"My doctor said I was in good shape and prescribed a small glass of wine before bedtime. I bought my first bottle of port just like I was filling a prescription. What happened to me after that was almost unbelievable.

"In January of that first year, I was choking down the wine like some disagreeable medicine. I didn't like it at all. But I began to sleep through the night. I was more rested and relaxed and began to enjoy my various activities even more. Soon my 'glass of wine' became two, then three or four. By May of the following year, I was shopping at five different grocery stores (Heaven forbid that anyone should see me enter a liquor store!) so that no one checker would see how much wine I was buying.

"By that time I had dropped out of most of my church activities, drifted away from my friends, and stopped visiting my children. If anyone called after eight in the evening, I wouldn't answer the phone for fear of slurring my words. If the caller asked later, I'd say I'd been out or in the shower. I drank mostly in the evening, but sometimes it would continue into the next day. Then I'd pretend to have a bad cold or a touch of the flu. I became such a liar. I was horrified at myself. If my children hadn't intervened, I'd probably be dead by now."

Nothing about this soft-spoken, dignified lady indicated that she went willingly into a life of sin and self-indulgence. This was not social drinking gone awry. Nor did it seem to be situational, or reactive, alcoholism—a deliberate effort to escape from one of life's crises. She had apparently done her grieving for her dead husband and gotten on with a life that she found satisfying.

A psychologist might say that deep-set problems contributed to Victoria's insomnia and that alcohol alleviated her subliminal pain in such a way as to create a craving for more relief. Perhaps so. We understand now that we are whole people and that many, if not most, of our ailments are psychosomatic. Medical science recognizes the interrelationship between our minds and our bodies. But adding Victoria's story to many other similar, though less dramatic, tales from other alcoholics I've known shows me that alcoholism is more than an emotional problem. There is something different in the physical makeup of the alcoholic.

"What does the medical community say?"

In search of more evidence to support the disease theory, I spent an afternoon at the university library. Here are some of the facts I found:

The American Medical Association defines alcoholism as

> an illness characterized by preoccupation with alcohol and loss of control over its consumption which usually leads to intoxication if drinking is begun; by chronicity; by progression; and by the tendency toward relapse. Typically associated with physical disability and impaired emotional, occupational, and/or social adjustments as a direct consequence.[1]

Preoccupation with alcohol, loss of control, progression—every point fit my experience and observation. For the AMA to call alcoholism an illness was a giant step, considering that just a few decades ago compulsive drinkers were judged "hopeless" by the frustrated doctors who attempted to help them. Years of research by a few dedicated medical men had preceded the American Medical Association's declaration.

Among the persistent pioneers in the field of alcoholism were doctors at the Yale Plan Clinics in New Haven and Hartford, Connecticut. Doctors at these clinics made their primary goal one of public education: *acceptance of alcoholism as a disease.*

Not until the medical community as a whole declared its agreement with that viewpoint would the general public—most importantly alcoholics themselves and their loved ones—follow suit. And not until individuals began to see themselves as sick, instead of sinful, could they overcome the stigma and admit to their drinking problems.

The birth of Alcoholics Anonymous in 1935 and the "miracle cures" that followed had the single greatest impact upon the research in progress. Doctors watched and learned.

In 1955, representatives of the American Medical Association addressed the Twentieth Anniversary Convention of AA. Harry M. Tiebout, psychiatrist and trailblazer in the study of alcoholism, said, with reference to that amazingly successful organization: "After years of butting my head against the problem of treating the alcoholic, I can now begin to hope."[2] Other doctors conceded that alcoholism was a deep-seated emotional illness that must be treated according to psychosomatic principles.

During the fifties, the AMA recognized alcoholism as an illness of the emotions, which it most certainly is. In the intervening years, great strides have been made toward identifying alcoholism as a disease with a definite physiological basis. Whether the ailing emotions are more involved with the onset or the perpetuation of the disease is a question for science to pursue and for us to ponder.

CLUES IN THE LABORATORY

The emotional dimension in alcoholism is probably easier to understand and accept than the physiological, but the evidence indicating specific physical differences in alcoholics mounts. Some studies have shown that alcoholics may lack a particular enzyme needed for the normal metabolism of ethanol.

Author-physicians Janice Keller Phelps and Alan E. Nourse describe addictive people as having a

> hidden, inborn, inherited metabolic error or flaw that affects the way their bodies metabolize carbohydrates. As a result of the hidden error, these people live with a continuing physiological hunger that addicting substances, including alcohol, can partially and temporarily satiate. Many, if not most, addicts also suffer some element of depression recognized or unrecognized, which seems to be relieved for a time and to some degree by use of addicting substances, including alcohol.[3]

They conclude that

> addictiveness is a physiologic condition that includes a dysmetabolism of sugar and some degree of genetic depression with adrenal dysfunction.[4]

I learned that our bodies are designed to produce natural opiate-like substances called *endorphins* and that these substances may be lacking in addictive people. Research suggests that we may have a malfunction of the "hypothalamic-pituitary-adrenal axis—the great inter-woven system of body-regulating hormones that not only affect carbohydrate metabolism, but also control other appetites, feelings of well-being, emotions, body urges, desires, and physiological hungers."[5]

One fascinating discovery involved a substance called tetrahydroisoquinoline (TIQ). A medical scientist doing cancer research was surprised to find TIQ in the fresh brain tissue of skid row winos. This substance was known to be a product of heroin breakdown, but these winos had not been near heroin. Further investigation confirmed that the TIQ was caused by the alcoholic's inability to eliminate all the toxins in the alcohol he drank.

When a person drinks alcohol, it is broken down by liver enzymes into acetaldehyde, a highly toxic substance. In a normal drinker this toxin is changed into acetic acid, then into carbon dioxide and water, which is eliminated through the kidneys and lungs. However, the alcoholic's body apparently lacks the ability to eliminate all of the acetaldehyde and a small amount of it goes directly to the brain. Here it goes through a complicated chemical process and winds up as TIQ.

The implications of this discovery are too broad and technical to relate here, but the following facts about TIQ are significant enough to repeat:

- TIQ *doesn't occur in the brain of the normal social drinker*, only in that of the alcoholic.
- TIQ was tested as a possible pain killer during the Second World War and rejected because it was *too highly addictive*.
- Rats that cannot otherwise be made to drink alcohol even in weak solution will immediately

> *choose alcohol over water* after a minute injection of TIQ.[6]

Commenting on this discovery, David Ohlms, psychiatrist and addiction specialist said:

> After hundreds of years of moral condemnation of the alcoholic, science is on the threshold of exorcising the mythic devils of addiction. After all, medical science has helped eliminate the myths and prejudice surrounding all kinds of historically misunderstood and despised diseases: epilepsy, leprosy and schizophrenia, to name just a few. It shouldn't surprise us when science turns demon rum into a natural allergy.[7]

There is some disagreement among scientific researchers as to the basic cause of addiction. Some accept the disease model of alcoholism but continue to believe that its cause is primarily psychological.

> Dr. James Milam has made a major contribution to the recognition of alcoholism as a PRIMARY physical disease. Dr. Milam has strongly asserted that psychological and social factors play no stronger role in alcoholism than in any other chronic disease. He has challenged the notion that alcoholism is caused by psychological susceptibility and presented the view that the body of the person who becomes addicted to alcohol does not react to alcohol in the same way as the person who does not become addicted.[8]

ETHNIC TRENDS

Lawrence Lumeng, a biochemist at the Indiana University School of Medicine, experienced a reaction to alcohol common to Asians known as "Oriental flush." He analyzed his own DNA in search of the reason for his intolerance to liquor. He found a "lazy enzyme" that interferes with the body's breakdown of alcohol. This condition allows the build-up of acetaldehyde, which causes reddened face, headaches, or nausea in many Asians. Lumeng and biochemist Ting-Kai Li pinpointed the gene that instructs cells to make the odd enzyme. He demonstrated that this negative physical reaction to alcohol was genetically dictated and thus "inherited as surely as eye color."[9]

Varying rates of alcoholism in other ethnic groups indicate an inherent susceptibility to the disease. People of Irish, German, and Nordic ancestry seem to have a greater susceptibility to alcoholism than the Oriental or Jewish races. The high rate of alcoholism among American Indians is well known. Although culture probably plays a role in these racial tendencies, there is clear indication that genetic factors are involved.

> The biological approach took a big step forward in April (1990), when researchers reported the identification of a specific gene that may play a key role in some forms of alcoholism as well as in other addictions. Of the alcoholics they studied, 77 percent had the gene. The discovery, announced by researchers at the University of Texas and UCLA, is a gene linked to the receptors for dopamine, a brain chemical involved in the sensation of pleasure. Such discoveries, scientists say, herald biological markers that may one day make possible early identification of those most at risk of becoming addicted, allowing more effective prevention or treatment.[10]

It becomes more and more obvious that some of us are genetically vulnerable to the disease of alcoholism. It is the predisposition coupled with the alcohol itself that points certain ones of us in the direction of disaster.

"Is alcoholism inherited?"

I hardly needed to consult the experts on this one. The great majority of alcoholics I have known (numbering in the hundreds over the past three decades) are children, grandchildren, nephews, or nieces of alcoholics. Some, I suspect, come from families where the skeletons have been so securely closeted that their addictive roots are unknown.

Statistics bear out my personal observations. Children of alcoholic parents are four times more likely than other children to become alcoholics themselves. Many studies have demonstrated the particular vulnerability of these children. C. Robert Cloninger, a psychiatrist and geneticist at Washington University in St. Louis, says, "What is inherited is not the fact that you are destined to become an alcoholic but varying degrees of 'susceptibility' to alcoholism."[11]

According to Phelps and Nourse, "Addictiveness is determined by the physiology and biochemistry a person inherits at birth." In addition they have found that alcoholics are prone to

> genetic depression: a chronic physiological and biochemical depression that is transmitted from generation to generation in some families, although not necessarily to every family member. It is closely related to addictiveness, possibly stemming from the same physiological defect.[12]

"What's more important—heredity or environment?"

"Isn't it logical," someone asked, "that growing up with the insecurity and chaos of an alcoholic home is the real reason alcoholic parents have alcoholic children?"

In other words, isn't it nurture rather than nature that makes the difference?

My father was an alcoholic. My son is an alcoholic. We each had that "x factor" among our inherited genes that made us vulnerable to the disease of alcoholism. In each of our cases, lifestyle and culture seemed to have had little to do with it.

My father's parents were strict Methodists and teetotalers. Dad grew up rather straight-laced—a hard-working, ultraconservative, law-abiding citizen, who respected the Prohibition laws. When that act was repealed, he joined his professional peers in an occasional cocktail, but his habitual drinking started late in life, after I'd grown and left home. Until he retired at seventy-five, no one who knew him would have suspected that he had a drinking problem. Even then only his wife and children saw the warning signs. When my mother died he lost most of the control he'd fought so hard to maintain and his addiction began to be noticeable to friends and neighbors. Dad's alcoholism developed slowly, but his private life was pretty much centered around alcohol by the time he died at eighty-eight.

My son, on the other hand, grew up with sober alcoholics. Ned was only eleven when his stepfather and I, both recovering alcoholics, were married. He and our other boys had a few adolescent flings that they confessed to later, but there were no indications of serious drinking problems. When Ned was thirty-six he astounded us with the announcement that he was an alcoholic. For years his lifestyle had centered around family and church, and we'd rarely seen him take a drink.

"Sure," said, "I'd have a cold beer with the guys after a baseball game or when someone came into the shop on a hot day. And if we have a special dinner party at someone's home, there's always wine on the table. We're Christians, but we don't have any legalistic stand against drinking in moderation."

Many sincere Christians feel the same. Unfortunately, Ned's occasional can of beer or glass of wine eventually triggered his dormant disease.

Another of our sons (Ned's stepbrother) began to show signs of a drinking problem shortly after high school. Despite our familiarity with the disease, we were blind to the symptoms of alcoholism in our own son. After three years in the service, he emerged a full-blown alcoholic. Later after some horrendous experiences, and by the grace of God, he became willing to enter a treatment program and is sober today.

Two of our nine children have inherited our disease of alcoholism, in line with statistical probabilities.

COMPLICATED CAUSES

Each of these young men had an alcoholic parent, an early childhood influenced by the insecurity and chaos of active alcoholism, and growing-up years in a household where we, as parents, were sober but (I realize now) still suffering from the effects of the illness we shared. Were the less-than-ideal conditions of childhood the predisposing factors of our sons' alcoholism, or was it the genes that we passed on to them? Or was it that they were both "middle" children, shy and sensitive by nature, perhaps overwhelmed by the maze of relationships in our large blended family?

There are no simple answers to those questions. Each individual is a unique combination of genes and personality traits, and even within the same family, each will have a different experience as he interacts with his parents, siblings, and environment. Many factors are involved in producing the syndrome of alcoholism, and in any given case, one factor may dominate.

Studies have shown that even when children of alcoholic parents are adopted at birth or raised in non-alcoholic foster homes they have an unusually high rate of alcoholism. Heredity seems to outweigh environment in these cases. All serious research seems to point to a physiological basis for alcoholism and to reinforce the disease theory. The "x factor" determines the physical vulnerability; a difficult family situation, poor environment, or undue stress may be the catalyst.

The *Alcohol and Drug Abuse Handbook* gives us a concise summary of the technical information on alcoholism.

> Although the etiology of alcoholism remains unknown, there is considerable evidence that it is multifactional in nature. More specifically, alcoholism, like other disease, is an interaction between an agent, a host, and the environment.[13]

I ended my day's research convinced that I am anatomically and functionally different from my non-alcoholic sister who is able to "handle" a bit of social drinking. With that conviction has come the freedom from guilt that allows me to identify myself as an alcoholic and to try to help others to understand the alcoholics in their lives.

"How can you tell a heavy drinker from an alcoholic?"

Heavy social drinkers and alcoholics look a lot alike. The following case histories show the similarity of outward symptoms between the two:

Warren Walker is a heavy drinker. He has two highballs every evening after work, sometimes three on Saturdays, and a few beers on Sunday while he's mowing the lawn. When he and his wife go out for dinner, they go to restaurants that serve cocktails. If his teetotaling Aunt Jane comes for a visit he will grumble and protest at missing his customary drinks, but accept his enforced temporary abstinence.

Chuck Owen is an alcoholic. His drinking habits appear to be almost precisely the same on a day-by-day basis as Warren's—this year. If you lived across the street from the Walker's and the Owen's homes, you might watch them sharing a beer on a Sunday afternoon and easily miss the subtle differences that make Warren a heavy drinker and Chuck an alcoholic.

Warren's drinking pattern has remained relatively constant over a period of several years; Chuck's has gradually escalated. He's taken to keeping an extra bottle of vodka in the garden shed for a quick pick-me-up. He refuses to attend non-drinking social events and discourages guests who won't join him in a martini. When his mother-in-law, who frowns on his drinking, is around, he spends a lot of time in the garden within easy reach of his cache.

Next year Warren's doctor may tell him to cut down

on the booze for his health's sake, and he will be able to drastically curtail his habit. If Chuck's doctor gives him the same advice, he *may* be able to quit altogether (and chances are he won't), but he won't be able to control his addiction enough to "cut down" for any significant length of time.

Warren has a habit; Chuck has an addiction. Warren has a desire to drink; Chuck has a compelling need for the drug ethanol. As time passes, they will become less and less alike.

ATYPICAL TYPES

It's not hard to spot an alcoholic on the skid rows of Chicago or Seattle or any other city on the continent. He's the derelict among derelicts, curled into a doorway, if he can find one, with dirty newspapers for bedding and an empty wine bottle in a brown paper bag at his elbow. He's the transient combing the local hobo jungle for empties, looking around furtively before he lifts the containers one after another to his lips. You may think of this unfortunate man as the "typical" alcoholic, but he is not. Only 3 percent of this country's alcoholics are on skid row. The rest are in city apartments, suburban neighborhoods, farming communities, at the checkstand in the local grocery store or climbing the corporate ladder downtown.

You may suspect alcoholism in a less obvious case—that woman down the street who drops plastic bags full of bottles into the park dumpster on her way to work. You know she backed into the Wilson's mailbox last week, and you read about her citation for drunk driving in the local sheriff's column. The neighbors whisper, "She's drunk again."

These are the people who have gone beyond heavy

drinking to a point where alcohol has become of primary importance in their lives. Your neighbor still has enough control over her life to keep a job and enough pride to hide her empty bottles, but her health is deteriorating and her home life is a disaster. The progression of the disease of alcoholism is inescapable. Without help she will eventually lose control of her circumstances and *could* end up on the street, another derelict.

Every alcoholic begins his drinking career with good intentions. If we had known what lay ahead, none of us would have taken the original first drink. By the time we suspected our own alcoholic tendencies it was too late; alcohol had become more important than life itself.

"What are the signs and symptoms of alcoholism?"

Identifying and diagnosing the disease of alcoholism in its early stages has baffled the medical profession and the families of problem drinkers for generations. Most of us fail to recognize alcoholism as the addiction process develops. Instead, we make our diagnosis when the disease is full blown and its complications can no longer go unheeded.

According to the American Psychiatric Association, there are eight symptoms that most frequently and consistently appear in the alcoholic.

1. **Preoccupation** with alcohol or the next opportunity to drink.
2. **Increased tolerance** for alcohol. The ability to drink a lot and still function relatively well. (Tolerance is a pharmacological phenomenon in which more and more alcohol is required to achieve the desired effect. Eventually this tolerance precludes alcohol from being

a truly workable and satisfactory drug for mood altering.)

3. **Gulping drinks.** Consuming the first one or two drinks fairly fast. Ordering doubles.
4. **Drinking alone.** This may include drinking in public places, but by oneself.
5. **Using alcohol as a medication.** For relief of tension or anxiety or as an aid to sleep.
6. **Blackouts.** Drinking quantities sufficient to cause amnesia during the drinking episode.
7. **Hiding bottles.** Having a bottle secreted in the home or elsewhere in case a drink is "needed."
8. **Non-premeditated drinking.** Drinking much more than anticipated or drinking differently than previously planned.[14]

I know of practicing alcoholics who have taken that test and "passed." They are relieved to be able to tell their families that they aren't alcoholic after all. The acceptable scores on their self-graded tests give them license to go on drinking a while longer.

The problem with lists of symptoms like that above is that they invite self-diagnosis, which is nearly always resisted by the alcoholic. In his desperation to deny the existence of a problem, he will refuse to recognize the danger signals. He will be able to conceal the signs of his addiction (the hidden bottle, the extra drinks, even the blackouts) from his bewildered loved ones long after he has crossed the line from social to alcoholic drinking. As long as he refuses to see himself as alcoholic he will be able to continue drinking. That he must continue to drink despite threats to job, health, and family is an all-encompassing symptom of his disease.

Alcoholics under the influence of alcohol tend to fantasize in such a way as to distort the reality of their lives. In so doing, significant insight is lost and the patient comes to believe that he or she does not have a drinking problem, it is being caused by some external factor; and if any intervention is required, it should be directed toward the thing or person responsible for the patient's drinking.[15]

I can relate to that. It was my failing marriage, my demanding children, outside pressures, and inside turmoil that caused me to drink too much. Little was known about alcoholism in the years when my disease was taking its toll on me and my family. I knew of a man who had declared himself an alcoholic and had quit drinking forever. I thought I would rather die than be in his shoes. *I'd rather die than quit drinking*, I thought. And but for the grace of God I would have.

SUMMARY

- Alcoholism is a disease by medical definition.
- Drunkenness is a sin committed involuntarily by alcoholics.
- Alcoholism happens to all kinds of people.
- The causes of alcoholism are complicated, but heredity is definitely a factor.
- There are more alcoholics in nice neighborhoods than on skid rows.
- Alcoholics and their families resist seeing the signs of their disease.
- An alcoholic would often rather die than quit drinking.

"Why Do You Want to Die?"

My friend Cindy leaned across the lunch table and lowered her voice. She'd agreed to share the story of her battle with alcoholism with me. Looking at this vibrant, attractive woman it was hard to believe that she'd once come close to drinking herself to death.

"You remember that in those days we were *conceding* that alcoholism might be a disease," she began, "but by that we meant it was an emotional problem. And behind that concept were all kinds of judgments—alcoholics were temperamentally unstable, weak-willed, low on coping skills, that kind of thing. It followed then that the psychological approach like counseling, psychoanalysis, bio-feedback, or hypnosis—anything to get at the inner person—was the right way to go for a cure. Some psychiatrists were even trying LSD on their patients in the sixties!

"My drinking had gotten steadily worse over a period of time, and our marriage was in shambles. I thought the

conflict at home was the *cause* instead of the *result* of my
alcoholism. Except I certainly didn't think of myself as an
alcoholic. My frantic husband thought I was going
through some kind of mental breakdown and he tricked
me into an appointment with a 'marriage counselor,'
thinking I could be charmed, reasoned, and psychoana-
lyzed out of my drinking problem in a few sessions of
counseling.

"Martin had the world's best intentions, but he had
no idea how desperately I'd hang on to the one thing in my
life that gave me pleasure. A few years later, as I was finally
sober and recovering, I tried to reconstruct that first
appointment in my journal. I was trying to understand the
craziness of my thinking at that stage of my disease. Here's
the scenario as I remembered and wrote it."

She slipped the worn journal into my hands. I opened
it tenderly, knowing I was going to peer into her pain. I
began to read the words she had written:

April 12, 1977. Three years today. Three years
since that spring morning when hope was born in my
heart and that awful winter was finally over. I was in
such an alcoholic fog that I don't remember much
about those days of my drinking—except for isolated
incidents, like burning the prime rib at Easter time
and being coerced into that disastrous appointment
with Martin's "marriage counselor." I remember Dr.
Page's first words to me:

"Cynthia," he said, "why are you trying to kill
yourself? What is it in your life that makes you so
unhappy?"

My mind flinched away from his question. I sat
very still in the brown leather chair across from
Winfield Page, Ph.D. I unlocked my eyes from his

steady gaze and looked around the small office. Dingy. I supposed the monochromatic color scheme was meant to be restful. Behind Win's desk and over his head hung an abstract painting in shades of gray. It blended well with the room and the January sky outside.

For the first ten minutes of my appointment we'd talked like new acquaintances at a cocktail party. He'd asked me to call him Win, then asked what I thought of the painting. Very casually. *He probably thinks I won't suspect he hung it there just for my benefit. Any dummy could see that light area around the frame where another picture was, maybe even this morning. I wonder if he has a selection—one for each category of patient: depressed, paranoid, neurotic, anxious, just plain whacko.*

I was suffering from anxiety, according to the good doctor. Free-floating anxiety, whatever that meant. My mind tended to float a bit at times like this, but there was nothing free about the way I felt.

The painting was supposed to be an ice-breaker, a conversation-opener.

"What do you see in that picture?" Win had asked.

A tune kept running through my head—*Buckle down, Winsocki.* I tried to concentrate.

What I saw was a jumble of lines and shapes, but I didn't want to irritate him right off, so I thought I'd better think of a better answer. The dark forms were obviously supposed to be wine bottles, one standing straight in the foreground, the rest lying flat, scattered along a kind of road that faded into some cloud shapes in the background.

Very clever. I wasn't going to walk into that trap.

"Tenpins, I think. Tenpins in a bowling alley." I made my eyes go wide and innocent.

I hadn't come there to talk about my drinking habits, but about my disintegrating marriage. Martin suggested it, after the first time the word "divorce" was spoken aloud between us. . . .

"Cynthia?" Dr. Page's voice pulled me back to his dreary little office. I wished he wouldn't call me Cynthia. No one did, except my mother. She said CYNthia, with the emphasis on the first syllable. When I was little I thought there was some connection between my name and "sin."

"Yes, I heard the question. Kill myself? I don't want to kill myself."

He's determined to talk about my drinking. Martin's doing, of course. My devoted husband blames all our problems on that. Ridiculous for them to decide behind my back that I'm trying to end my life when all I've ever wanted to do was live.

I'd found the secret to life a long time ago, when I was a freshman at college, away from home for the first time and scared spitless of everything. My clothes were all wrong, my roommate didn't like me, the classes I wanted were full, and the one weekend I'd counted on going home Mom called and said they were going on a golfing junket to Carmel with Dad's buddies.

Everyone around me in the dorm seemed to be having so much *fun*, and that night they were talking about driving out to Santa Monica for a beach party. I needed to wash my hair, and I didn't want to go, but I wanted to stay in the dorm alone even less. My roommate, Diane, was one of those all-out extroverts who made me feel like a prize dud, but she decided to take me under her wing and drag me along with her boyfriend and his fraternity brother with the brillo-pad hair.

"A blind date," she said. "His name's Fred, and the guys say he's a lot of fun."

I didn't fit. For a while everyone raced up and down the beach, playing tag and shrieking like twelve-year-olds at a slumber party. I kind of stood on the fringe and pretended to laugh at their antics. Afterward they built a fire and sat around talking in that sophisticated way that college students have, competing to see who could spout the most philosophical jargon. Psychobabble. They buried their cigarette butts in the sand and passed around a bottle of Jack Daniels that my "lot-of-fun date" had brought. I'd had a couple of those fancy mixed drinks on my high school graduation night, and I kind of liked the feeling but hated the taste of alcohol, even when it was mixed with coke or ginger ale. How could they drink the stuff straight?

As the bottle came closer and closer to my place in the circle I tried to formulate an escape plan. I could slip out and go up to the restroom by the sea wall, but the little building looked pretty dark and lonely, so I decided to just put the bottle to my lips and fake it when it came to me. Everyone was wrapped up in themselves and their brilliant conversation, anyway, so no one would notice. That's what I thought.

"Oh, come on, Cindy. Don't be such a prude! This is real good, smooth stuff. It might loosen you up a little." Diane patted me on the head like I was a cocker spaniel.

Now everyone was looking, so I forced a laugh and took a deep swig. It felt warm going down. "Hey," I said. "Not bad. Anybody got a beer chaser?" One clown doubled up laughing and put his face right in the sand. Someone ran up to the parking lot and

came back with a six-pack. I like beer even less than
bourbon, but I couldn't back out then.

Fun-Freddy popped the tab for me and handed me
the can with a look of approval. "You're a riot, you
know it? One of those dead-pan comedians. How
come you've been hiding that sense of humor all
night?"

"Okay everyone," Diane bubbled, "the party can
begin. Cindy's come to life!"

I didn't know what I'd said that was so funny, but
all of a sudden I belonged, I was among friends, and
Freddy wasn't half bad looking. It was all connected
to the booze. That beach party left me with an
afterglow instead of a hangover, and it left me with an
eternal thirst for more.

*That, Doctor Win-Sockey, is my secret, and I'm not
telling you. My happy button is buried deep down in
my gut somewhere, and booze is the trigger. I'm not
giving it up for you or Martin or anyone else. If you
think that's trying to kill myself, so be it.*

I looked up from the handwritten pages that Cindy
had brought to share with me. We were, I'd thought, as
different as any two women could be. She, slim, blond and
beautiful, vivacious and outgoing; me, well, pretty much
the opposite. Yet she'd told a story that could so easily
have been my own.

"I was *so* defensive," she was saying, blushing a little
as she returned the journal to her purse. "I built a wall
between the good doctor and myself brick by brick, just as
I'd done with Martin and my parents and our friends. I
sabotaged everyone's attempts to reach me. Booze began
by freeing me up to relate to people and ended by locking
me in a walled prison. I thought in my insanity that I was

clutching at life, but in reality I was on a fast track toward death."

Most of us have felt the same way. Alcohol had done something wonderful for us in the beginning, but somewhere along the line, it had begun to kill us.

"Does the alcoholic really want to die?"

Mental health professionals tell us that a subconscious "death wish" is involved with our continued drinking, that it is the basis for all self-destructive behavior. Alcoholism, they say, is the manifestation of self-hate turned inward. Most of us weren't aware of that. We thought we were looking for happiness as we damaged our livers, increased our risk of miocardial disease and high blood pressure, burned our stomach linings, and disrupted our immune systems. All we wanted was that elusive "good feeling" we'd had in the beginning.

As euphoria continues to elude us, some of us deliberately choose the ultimate escape. According to statistics, the alcoholic is thirty times more likely to commit suicide than the non-alcoholic. Intentionally or not, we are killing ourselves (and too often our loved ones) at an alarming rate. A recent issue of *U.S. News & World Report* says:

> Alcohol is a factor in nearly half of America's murders, suicides and accidental deaths. In all, it claims at least 100,000 lives per year, 25 times as many as all illegal drugs combined. That's the government's estimate, based largely on death certificates.[1]

That estimate is almost certainly low, as many death certificates give no clue to alcohol's role in an individual's death.

Research has consistently demonstrated that alcohol is directly or indirectly responsible for the hospitalization of as many as 25–30% of the patients on general medical wards, and yet the diagnosis of alcoholism is disproportionately under-represented on the medical records. Physicians are reluctant to record a diagnosis of alcohol abuse or alcohol dependence, even when there is little doubt about the patient's alcoholism.[2]

LOST INCENTIVE

An elderly relative of mine—Uncle Jim, I'll call him—fought his disease of alcoholism for years before he died of what his death certificate called "arteriosclerosis." Jim was an ambitious and energetic businessman and, over the years before his retirement, had risen to a position near the top of his company. His drinking then was confined to the customary business lunches with clients, an occasional social gathering with friends and neighbors, and his usual before-dinner cocktail at home. When he retired at sixty-five—reluctantly and only because of company policy—his drinking habits changed along with his daily schedule.

Accustomed to drinking at lunchtime, he would emerge from his den at noon to mix himself a highball. But, without the pressure of having to return to the office, he would often have two or three while he and Aunt Mabel ate their lunch. Often he fell asleep over a book in the afternoon. When Mabel protested that he was "sleeping the day away," he switched to wine, drank one glass at lunchtime, and busied himself at his workbench in the garage for the afternoon. Sometimes a neighbor would stop by to chat or someone from his company would call with a problem, and he would change into his business suit and go into town.

It was a long time before Mabel discovered the wine bottle in the cabinet behind the paint thinner. When she confronted him, he insisted that he only kept the wine there for the sake of neighborly hospitality. He told her that when someone stopped in to look at his latest project, he didn't like to come tracking dirt into the house to get something out of the refrigerator. Mabel didn't particularly like the idea of his keeping wine in the workshop but since Jim never appeared "drunk," she let it go.

Jim could be called a "plateau" drinker, having enough control to space his drinks throughout the day. In that way he was able to keep his blood-alcohol level fairly constant. With little outward evidence of drunkenness, even Aunt Mabel and close family members failed to realize the extent of his problem. But after Mabel died, Jim seemed to give up the fight to maintain his dignity. He was in his eighties by that time and had moved to a retirement home. He had lost contact with his company (although he had his old business card taped to the door of his apartment), his friendly neighbors had scattered and gotten out of touch, and his failing hearing prevented him from communicating easily with others in the retirement home.

DEATH BY DEFAULT

He began drinking more carelessly in the weeks before his death and his nieces reported to each other that he sounded "out of it" when they telephoned any time after noon. The manager mentioned one day that Jim had started picking up something from the local delicatessen and eating alone in his room instead of joining the others for dinner in the community dining room.

I knew, and his physician may have known, that his episodes of dizziness and his frequent falls were directly related to his intake of alcohol. If anyone suggested that he might "cut down" a little, he was offended and defensive. Indeed, the niece who was most concerned gained the reputation of "nag" among family members.

"Oh, let the old man alone," one of his nephews had said as his cousin deplored Jim's drinking habits. "At his age he has the right to enjoy himself." Perhaps only another alcoholic could have seen the lack of joy in Uncle Jim's life during those final months. His was not a deliberate suicide, but a death by default. Grief and loneliness undergirded the alcoholism that caused his death.

Alcoholism among our elderly is not uncommon. Author and playwright Larry King writes of the problem among his "sixtyish" peers:

> Those who have *not* made positive choices [about lifestyles] are, almost to the last in number, practicing alcoholics—as I was until a bit more than six years ago. I can only think of them as pitiful cases of arrested emotional development, though I know alcoholism is a disease, the same as cancer or glaucoma. Strangely, many of these seem to fear death beyond reason, as if a world without them is too horrible to be contemplated, though one who has himself walked in the dark valley of alcoholism cannot help but regard them as already among the living dead: Perpetual fogs and bouts of oblivion are not key ingredients in the chemistry of life. They are, rather, tools for premature burials.[3]

IGNORING THE WARNINGS

Like Cynthia, the alcoholic refuses to heed any warnings that he may be killing himself, that getting sober is a matter of life and death. "I'm not *that* bad," he protests. Or, "Look at Al Parker, he drank every day until he was ninety-five and died from a fall off his tractor!"

The National Council on Alcoholism gives us these startling statistics:

- Alcoholism is the third leading cause of death in the U.S.
- Alcoholism is considered the number one medical problem by the U.S. Public Health Service.
- Alcoholism is the fourth leading medical problem in the world, according to the World Health Organization.
- Every twenty-three minutes someone in the United States loses his life to a drunk driver.
- Twenty-five teenagers die daily from alcohol.
- Sixty-three percent of all patients in veterans' hospitals are there for liquor related reasons.
- Cirrhosis of the liver is the nation's seventh biggest killer. Ninety percent of its victims are alcoholics. One out of ten alcoholics develops cirrhosis.

These facts are put before the newspaper-reading, television-watching public over and over again, but the drinking alcoholic refuses to see or hear them. Even if he is aware of his own physical decline or his risk of accidental death, he feels powerless to prevent the inevitable.

One alcoholic said of himself:

I knew that something was very wrong with me. I even knew I was an alcoholic, but I had long since come to believe that there was nothing I could do about it. I had decided it was perfectly appropriate— just fine—that I should die. In fact, I honestly hoped that I would, sparing further grief for many people I loved. Dying, I thought, was the best thing I could ever do for them. The idea of living without alcohol never occurred to me. I preferred the idea that I was a hopeless case.[4]

RUNNING OUT OF HOPE

There are crossovers between the suicidal person and the alcoholic that may further confuse the statistics. When "hitting bottom" involves more despair than hope, the alcoholic's subconscious death wish may surface and result in deliberate suicide.

Gordon was forty-one years old when his wife, Donna, left him for the third time because of his drinking. Gordon pulled himself together, began attending AA meetings, and stopped hanging around the local tavern with his friends after work. He told his new friends at AA that he was sure Donna would come back when she saw that he'd stopped drinking. They told him that he had to stay sober for himself, not for anyone else. Gordon sometimes felt misunderstood when he talked at AA meetings.

Eventually he started stopping at the tavern again "just to see old Bob and have a laugh or two." He drank plain tonic water while his friends had their beers. But it wasn't the same, and usually he'd go home more depressed than before. One night he called Donna about some papers that had to be signed, and a man answered the phone. When Donna came to the phone, she said she was filing for divorce. When he told her he'd been sober for three months, she congratulated him. When he said he'd like to get together for a talk, she said she didn't think they had anything to talk about.

Gordon went out and bought a bottle of vodka, which he began to drink on the way home. Afterwards, sitting in the car with the garage door closed behind him and the engine running, he finished the bottle. His neighbor found him there the next afternoon. His death, like many others, was a direct result of his alcoholism, although the statistical record will show him as a suicide.

"Why couldn't he ask for help?"

Perhaps the difference in the progression toward death by alcoholism and death by deliberate suicide is that the suicidal person usually reaches out for help in some way. He probably won't ask directly but instead will give clues of his intentions by his behavior or in offhand remarks to those around him. He may say things like, "You'd be better off without me." Or "You won't have to worry about me much longer." He may suddenly make a will or put his affairs in order as if he were getting ready to go on a long trip. Almost all people planning suicide make some attempt to communicate with significant other people in their lives before killing themselves.

The alcoholic, on the other hand, will go to any lengths to cover his tracks. If he puts up a good front, he thinks, "they" won't start lecturing him about his drinking again. Of course, his uncontrolled drinking will not stay under cover for long. It is in itself a cry for help. The alcoholic wants help desperately, but only if that help doesn't interfere with his drinking.

Both the deliberately suicidal person and the alcoholic will behave in ways that elicit responses of anger or rejection, rather than sympathy, from those around them. While the suicidally depressed person is expected to "snap out of it" or "look on the bright side," the alcoholic is admonished to "use a little self-discipline."

Overtaxed friends and families can't be blamed for their intolerance. To live with someone who is unpredictable, inconsistent, and unreliable is a difficult burden for all members of the family, even if they understand that such behavior is the result of illness. But every negative response from those around the sick person is like the blow of a hammer, driving him further into his disease. The vicious cycle is difficult to break.

THE RELUCTANT ACCOMPLICE

One young woman said, "I got tired of watching Ken killing himself and making me an accomplice. As long as I continued to stay with him, we got nowhere with his drinking problem. I say 'we,' because I'd made it my problem, too. Every time he came in the door drunk, my resolutions about keeping my cool went down the drain. I either lost my temper or ended up in tears, and that just made things worse between us. He had a way of twisting things around so my reaction was the *reason* for the next drunk! He said, 'Being married to a hysterical woman would drive any man to drink.' Or, 'If I could have a little peace when I come home after a hard day, maybe I wouldn't drink so much.' On the rare occasions when I tried to force myself to be understanding, I was 'psychoanalyzing' him!

"As long as we stayed together I reacted badly and he had me to blame for his drinking. Now that we're separated, he'll have to find someone else to blame. This is just one more crisis in our lives that Ken and his drinking have brought on. I hope he's able to see that before he drinks himself to death. If so, our separation may help to save his life."

ESCAPING FROM REALITY

For both the alcoholic and the non-alcoholic suicidal person, one crisis seems to follow another. The latter comes to a point where he is barely coping with the problems of daily life. His stress level is low because of the wearing-down effect of unhappy experiences. He is chemically depressed or genetically fragile. At any rate, one more straw upon the camel's back will overwhelm him and he will begin to contemplate the ultimate escape—death.

The alcoholic comes to the same crisis point, has a drink or two (in the beginning of his drinking career) and discovers that the stress of whatever burdens he is carrying eases considerably. (There is evidence that the alcoholic feels a higher "high" than the normal drinker.)

As his illness of alcoholism progresses, it takes more and more alcohol to have an effect. He usually discovers that he can't recapture the euphoria that he found in the beginning. His goal, unconscious or not, has been a partial escape from reality, an easing of the pressure he feels. But he can no longer stop at a drink or two. The first few drinks offer him no relief and the next lead him to a state of drunkenness. Somehow he misses the in-between stage, the sought-after glow.

The alcoholic's overindulgence compounds any problems and personality scars that existed before he began to drink. His stress level goes down, his coping skills diminish, his life is falling apart around him. He returns to a crisis point more and more frequently. Now he chooses to anesthetize himself with alcohol rather than face stark reality. His body is still alive, but he has barricaded his mind and emotions from the pain of living.

"What can we do to stop him?"

Begin with prayer and the acceptance of alcoholism as a disease. While alcohol blinds your alcoholic to the reality that he may be drinking himself to death, you and others who care for him may be fighting your own battles with denial. The more aware you are of the problem, the more ready you will be to help when the time comes.

RESCUE ATTEMPTS

"I called our family doctor after Arnie had his annual checkup," said my friend Claire. "He has high blood pressure, and he'd promised me that he'd clear his evening cocktails—at least two martinis every day—with Dr. Cowan, but of course he didn't. What he said was, 'Is it okay if I have a drink now and then, Doc?' Dr. Cowan said it is downright dangerous for Arnie to keep drinking so heavily, but he can't do anything unless Arnie is willing to talk about it."

To stand by quietly while someone drinks alcoholically is like watching helplessly as a blind man teeters on the edge of a cliff. We want to rescue the unwary victim. At the same time we are apt to be angry at the endangered one for wandering away from middle-of-the-road safety and involving us in his perilous situation. If we get too close, we may go over the edge with him. Our inclination is to shout a warning, or at least "talk some sense into" the one threatening to fall, but we'd better get a rope around him first.

The drinking alcoholic will be unable to hear admonitions, warnings, or appeals to his common sense as long as his mind and body scream with the compelling need for another drink. The alcoholic may be mentally and emotionally ill and in desperate need of psychiatric care, but unless the pattern of drinking is interrupted long enough for him to see his own need, there is little hope for enduring sobriety.

Like the blind man, what the alcoholic needs is to be rescued before he goes beyond the point of no return. Once rescued from the physical addiction, he can be helped to clear his mind enough to work on problems of soul and spirit. But an alcoholic can't be helped until he "hits bottom," recognizes his plight, and is willing to accept help. The prevailing theory has been that nothing could be done for the alcoholic until he somehow, on his own, arrived at this necessary turning point. The "rescue" his loved ones prayed for hung by some thread of fate or depended upon miraculous intervention.

THE HOUND OF HEAVEN

Miracles happen every day in the lives of alcoholics, and there is no more convincing intervention than the one some of us have experienced: the sudden awareness of God's presence and the desire to follow Him. That happened to me, and it happened to Cindy, whose story follows:

"My miracle happened on that April morning when I finally decided to call for help. I look back on that as a time of spiritual awakening. In reality I awoke in my own bedroom with four-year-old Mandy peering over the edge of my bed, her chin resting on the crumpled sheets and her little face close to mine. I couldn't focus well enough to read the time on the bedside clock, but I could see the dirt on Mandy's face and knew that I'd put her to bed without a bath again. She'd tried to dress herself but couldn't find any clean clothes, so she had on some ragged jeans that were too small. I knew without looking that Jennifer and Lisa had gotten themselves off to school, probably without breakfast.

"It certainly wasn't the first morning I'd awakened to a scene like that, but somehow on that particular day I really *saw* myself. It was like I was standing in the doorway looking down at the pathetic woman I'd become. Besides that, I had a strong impression that God was standing beside me, ready to help me face the mess I'd made of my life. And instead of drowning my remorse in the bottle that day, I picked up the phone and called AA.

"Oh, I was a long time getting well, but from that morning on I felt *hope* and a kind of inner joy because I knew God was really real. Later when I read the story of the Prodigal Son in the book of Luke I wanted to shout, 'That's me! That's me!' I was the prodigal daughter who came to her senses in the pigpen and began the long journey home."

Each of us must come to our moment of truth and "hit bottom," as we alcoholics say. But there are things that our loved ones can do to speed the process. We'll explore those ways in later chapters.

"Will counseling help?"

Many people believe that getting to the reason for the alcoholic's drinking should be the first step in helping him. Alcoholism, like every other addiction, is a symptom of underlying causes, both physical and emotional.

When the psychologist asked Cynthia why she wanted

to die, he was saying, "What is it that hurts you so badly that you can't face living?" But Cynthia couldn't have told him, even if she'd been willing to cooperate. She had buried the source of her pain so thoroughly and anesthetized herself against its effects so well that no amount of therapeutic probing could reveal the secrets that she'd kept, even from herself. Although she didn't realize it, alcohol was her escape from life, from the pain she held deep within her. Consequently, it appeared that she was choosing to drink herself to death.

FIRST THINGS FIRST

Sobriety—abstinence from alcohol—must be the beginning of the road to recovery. Until the alcoholic sees that he has lost control of his life through his excessive drinking, he cannot begin to get well.

Most of us find our first days of sobriety both terrible and wonderful. There are the inescapable symptoms of physical withdrawal from our drug habit and the mental anguish of remorse for the hurt we've inflicted upon those who care about us. We would be overwhelmed were it not for that feeling of hope that Cynthia referred to. In the beginning we must focus on the present and leave the past and the future in God's hands. Our only task is to maintain the new and tender sobriety that we have found. There will be time enough for introspection and the search for root causes of our alcoholism.

Dr. Joseph Pursch, noted for his work with Betty Ford, believes group therapy with other addicted persons is the most effective for the alcoholic. There the emphasis is on current living problems as participants share their experiences in a world without alcohol. He says the alcoholic should first learn to live without alcohol or other drugs for at least a year

> before he climbs on the psychoanalytic wagon in search of why he was drinking. You don't look for the cause of the fire when the building is ablaze; and you don't teach navigation from the deck of a sinking ship.[5]

GROWING PAINS

Some characteristics are found to be common among chemically dependent people. You will probably recognize at least some of them in the alcoholic in your life. Remember that most of them have been caused or exaggerated by his disease. They are:

- emotional immaturity
- low tolerance for frustration
- inability to express emotions
- excessive dependency
- a high level of anxiety in interpersonal relationships
- perfectionism
- compulsiveness
- grandiosity

Most of these were rooted in childhood and have come into full flower as we drank alcoholically. These same character traits will stand in our way as we strive for a firm footing in the world of sobriety. We need to deal with each of them as they arise in our day-to-day lives and bring them under control before we dig deeper into the buried past. Every effective program of recovery will provide the alcoholic with tools for growth in these areas and with caring, supportive people on whom to practice our developing skills.

Eventually, however, we will need to face the "monsters of the deep"—those anxieties, fears, and guilts that lurk in our subconscious and may keep us from becoming the people God created us to be.

"Once he's sober, won't everything else take care of itself?"

If our alcoholism is arrested and there is no further therapy we may very likely become addicted to something else. We will continue to seek an escape from the pain of living, and we will utilize any device that works.

Dinah B., a recovering alcoholic with five years of sobriety, said, "The first couple of months that I was sober were wonderful. I felt like a new person, and I thought the future would take care of itself. Then I gradually started slipping back into my old habit patterns—watching too many soap operas, going on little eating binges, pouting and giving Jerry the silent treatment when I didn't get my way.

"I'd been going to AA meetings, just sitting there basking in my sobriety, but I thought those twelve steps that the program uses were an unnecessary gimmick. My only problem, I thought, was that I drank too much. Now that that was behind me, I was fine. One night someone at the meeting told me I'd better start working the program. He said the steps were there for a reason and I'd better get with it."

It's not surprising that we have work to do. Our natural maturing process was interrupted when we began to use alcohol as an escape. We can't go back, but we can start where we are and finish growing up.

ON THE RIGHT ROAD

Most of us had no desire to die, at least in the beginning of our drinking careers. We wanted to live more abundantly and thought we'd found the way. We wanted to deaden the pain of guilt, fear, anxiety, grief, and stress. We got off on the wrong road, trying to take a detour around life's jolts and bumps. It wasn't the easy way we thought and we've lost a lot of ground, but we're back on the main road now and ready to go forward. Our road to recovery will be a lifelong process.

As we clear away the mental cobwebs, heal physically, and grow spiritually, we will come to understand the true secret of abundant life. We can say with Paul, "I have been crucified with Christ and I no longer live, but Christ lives in me. The life I live in the body, I live by faith in the Son of God, who loved me and gave himself for me" (Gal. 2:20). And we can read the promise of our Lord, "The thief comes only to steal and kill and destroy; I have come that they may have life, and have it to the full" (John 10:10).

SUMMARY

- Some psychiatrists and psychologists say that alcoholics have a hidden death wish.
- Alcoholics are unable to see that they might be killing themselves.
- An alcoholic is thirty times more likely to commit suicide than a non-alcoholic.
- At least 100,000 people die each year from alcohol-related causes.
- Alcohol is the third leading cause of death in the United States.
- Alcohol is directly or indirectly responsible for the hospitalization of 25–30 percent of the patients on general medical wards.
- An alcoholic needs to be sober to benefit from counseling.
- Alcoholics have some common character traits that may stand in the way of their recoveries.

"Where Did We Go Wrong?"

The book of Proverbs gives us these words of wisdom: "Train a child in the way he should go, and when he is old he will not turn from it" (Prov. 22:6). We Christian parents believe that verse and we try to raise our children accordingly..We set their tender feet upon a path paved with our Christian values and trust that they will not stray from it. What goes wrong when our children take dangerous detours or openly rebel against our guidance?

"I don't know what's happened to Kevin," sobbed Julie Cooper. "Tim and I did everything we could to give our kids a good start in life. Neither of us grew up with the advantages that we were able to give our children. We loved them, we disciplined them, we gave them piano lessons and ski trips and encouragement in everything they did. Honestly, I thought we were great parents! Mark and Lisa have turned out to be wonderful young adults and have given us nothing but pleasure, but Kevin has been a problem ever since high school."

"Kevin was always a little different from the other two, though," Julie's husband, Tim, added. "As a little kid he'd get frustrated and lose his temper over some insignificant thing like whose turn it was to ride in the front seat. But I never thought he'd turn into an alcoholic. We must have failed with him somewhere along the line."

"What went wrong?"

It is devastating to watch an adolescent or adult child caught in the downward spiral of alcoholism. We add to our pain when we ask, "Where did we go wrong in our parenting? Couldn't we have prevented this disastrous turn of events?"

The answer is, probably not. Alcoholism, as we have seen, is a complex illness of the body, mind, and spirit. The alcoholic is predisposed to his disease, physically and emotionally. That is, the many facets of his personality are so arranged that he is particularly vulnerable to the disease of alcoholism. He is born that way. Given his predisposition and adding to that the ordinary lumps and bumps of childhood, he is more likely than another to become a victim of alcoholism.

PERSONALITY POTENTIALS

Sharon Wegscheider, alcoholism specialist and family therapist, identifies six distinct personal "potentials" that make up the whole person. They are: physical, emotional, social, mental, spiritual, and volitional. She compares the healthy person to a geometric circle, with each of these "potentials" occupying a separate but equally important segment of the whole.

> When any one [potential] is incomplete or dam-
> aged, the entire circle loses its integrity. . . . Each
> personal potential, though distinct, is in dynamic
> contact with every other, affecting and being affected
> constantly. If we imagine for a moment that the circle
> is a wheel, it becomes clear what a strong effect
> deformity in one segment can have on the function-
> ing of the whole. In any given real-life situation our
> feelings and behavior are the result of several, or even
> all six, of the potentials interacting in various propor-
> tions.[1]

There is infinite variety to be found within those six
potentials. That's what makes each of us a unique human
being. From the moment of birth, these elements of our
personalities are acted upon—strengthened or diminished—by the environment into which we are born.

A newborn infant, then, is a miraculous bundle of
potential, coming into the lives of two fallible people. He is
like a little computer, ready for programming. That is a
tremendous responsibility—one for which none of us is
adequate. God knows our insufficiency. He knows that in
our struggle with the assignment of parenthood many of us
will be drawn closer to Him. And in future years, as our
children strive to recover from the wounds of their
childhood, they too may turn to Him for healing.

Julie and Tim were good parents. Their two "successes" are a credit to them. But it is unrealistic to expect
even the most mature and devoted parents to avoid
mistakes. Kevin was probably put together in such a way
that his parents' mistakes, along with the other hurts of
childhood, left bruises upon his personality. Perhaps on
the day that he had his first drink of alcohol those bruises

were particularly tender. Maybe he felt a sense of relief from pain that he had never experienced before. That kind of positive experience laid the groundwork for future episodes of drinking. At some point, if not at the beginning, the physiological flaw that determined his physical addiction to alcohol came into play.

Kevin's alcoholism is not his parents' fault. They, like most parents, did the very best they could with each of their children. Kevin's physical and psychological make-up, together with the circumstances of his life, pointed him in the direction of the addictive drinker. His physical and psychological make-up, together with outside circumstances, will also determine whether he recovers from or is defeated by his disease.

PHYSIOLOGICAL FLAWS

Duane L. has a background of childhood neglect and abuse. His addictive drinking is understandable (and even forgivable) to anyone who knows his past history. "What can you expect?" his neighbors ask. "With a family like that, I'd drink too!" There are many alcoholics like Duane. But researchers have found that his twin, David, rescued from the same environment by adoption at birth, is also an alcoholic. David's loving adoptive parents helped him to develop self-esteem and strength of character, but their nurturing couldn't negate the physiological flaw that predisposed him to the disease of alcoholism.

Many parents of problem drinkers carry a burden of guilt, knowing the sins of omission and commission in their parenting. Our guilt is nonproductive. We must remember that we were no more responsible for our child's alcoholism than the parents of a diabetic are responsible for his disease.

A PARENT'S PAIN

I, as a mother of alcoholic sons, can't turn back the clock and apply acquired wisdom to years gone by. I can treasure God's promise that He makes all things work together for good for those who love Him (Rom. 8:28). Long ago each of these young men accepted God's gift of salvation through Jesus Christ. I believe they will one day allow Him to be Lord of their lives again. We are God's family, and His promise is our hope.

But, precious as that promise is, it doesn't take away the agony of *now!* In the lonely hours of the night, I'm startled awake by the vision of my child in danger. It doesn't matter that the "child" is a man of thirty-six with a family of his own and a life that doesn't include me. There are deep emotional ties between us that can't be denied. His entrance into adulthood didn't remove the maternal instinct that was born in me at his conception. He is the son that God gave me to love. I yearn to guide and protect him.

To those of us who are recovering alcoholics (and because of the heredity factor, many of us are) it is especially agonizing to watch a son or daughter in the trap of alcoholism. We've been there, and we remember the pain. We look back in wonder and gratitude at the miracle that released us from our addiction and is helping us to recover from our disease. Can we expect a miracle for our child? How much more will he have to suffer before he comes to that necessary point of surrender? What is happening to his family—the daughter-in-law I love and my precious grandchildren—every day that he continues to drink? Will this misery go on from generation to generation? Why can't he learn from our experiences?

We pray for God's intervention, yet we know that God will not interfere with our child's free will. And no one knows better than we do how strong is the will of an alcoholic whose only desire is to continue drinking!

I have valid reason for the remorse I feel over my inadequate parenting. I don't need to ask, "Where did I go wrong?" I'm painfully aware of the answers. My alcoholism left scars upon our entire family. But guilt is a crippling emotion. There is enough agony involved in watching our children suffer without rubbing the salt of self-condemnation into our wounds.

All of us have been shaped and molded by our childhood experiences. Our parents, our siblings, our peers, and our culture have all contributed to the people we are today. We can take some of the pressure off of ourselves and our parental failings as we look at society's influence on our children.

"Does our culture encourage drinking?"

Most people in our society drink alcoholic beverages at least occasionally. Unfortunately, young people usually have their first experience with alcohol during their high school years, if not earlier. A recent news article reported that two of every three high school seniors have drunk alcohol within the past month. Five percent drink daily. Forty percent of sixth-graders have tasted wine coolers.[2]

These young people are the least likely of any age group to drink alcohol responsibly, whether or not they have the physical predisposition for alcoholism. Remember those character traits that are common to alcoholics: emotional immaturity, excessive dependency, anxiety in interpersonal relationships, etc.? Now think about the teenagers you know. The emotional predisposition for problem drinking is almost automatic for teens.

Thousands of kids in hundreds of public and private schools are in trouble with alcohol. It has been called the "number one hard drug in America." And yet

- The liquor, wine, and beer industry spends over $900 million per year on advertising.
- There were over 600 beer commercials on television one New Year's Day for the five different bowl games.
- By age eighteen a child will have seen 100,000 beer commercials.

Our culture encourages and endorses the use of alcohol. As a nation and as a society we close our eyes to the frequently publicized fact that about one of every ten individuals who drink alcohol will become alcoholic. Since 95 percent of high school seniors drink, that is almost one tenth of the graduating class in your local high school.

PROBLEMS OF IMMATURITY

More and more young people in their teens and early twenties are coming to the meetings of Alcoholics Anonymous, many of them sent there by the courts. However, the same immaturity that speeds the progression of alcoholism in one predisposed to the disease may also stand in the way of his recovery.

"The DWI program in our city makes it mandatory for anyone caught 'driving under the influence' to attend six AA meetings," explained Betty Warden. "The trouble is that kids at that stage of life can't relate to the alcoholics they meet there. Our son Lance insisted that his arrest was just bad luck. 'Everyone drinks,' he said. 'We're no different from you and most of your adult friends, except that the cops are laying for us—waiting for us to make a wrong move. You know that old George Hadley drives around these streets loaded sometimes, and the cops look the other way. Now *there's* an alcoholic!'

"I had a hard time arguing with him," Betty continued. "He's right about some of that. And, I'm ashamed to say it, but we *do* drink and drive. My husband and I attend a lot of social things where alcohol is served, and one of us drives home. It's a case of knowing that we probably shouldn't but doing it anyway. The trouble with the young kids is they seem to set out to get drunk when they drink."

"Does that mean they're alcoholic?"

Only time will tell if they have the disease of alcoholism. According to a number of studies, most people who abuse alcohol or drugs in their teens and early twenties level off to social drinking by their early thirties. Even so, every day twenty-five teenagers across the country die in some alcohol-related way—usually in an automobile accident. Whether or not they were destined to be alcoholics, they are dead from alcohol.

EARLY WARNINGS

"I thought it was a lot of hogwash, sending Doug to those AA meetings because he got a ticket for having an open container in his car," said Leonard, a middle-aged executive. "Where did they get off putting my kid in a category with those drunks? I didn't stop to think that 'those drunks' were sober while my son was out drinking and getting into trouble with the law!

"It took us five years after that first incident to accept

the fact that Doug was really an alcoholic. We kept getting him out of scrapes and paying his fines and letting him snow us about how it was never his fault. Finally he was in an accident that was *obviously* his fault and the kid with him was almost killed. We had to face what was happening then. But we couldn't get Doug to face it."

"I cried myself to sleep night after night," said Doug's mother. "I was *so* frightened that he would kill himself or someone else. He lost his girlfriend and then his job, and he was devastated, but he couldn't see that it was his drinking that was wrecking his life. My heart ached for him in his misery, and not being able to help him was agonizing. Thank goodness someone directed us to a group of people who understood. It helped so much to talk to someone who had gone through the same thing with their child. I think it saved our sanity."

"Isn't there something else we can do?"

"One of the hardest things about watching an adult child suffer is that you can't *do* anything," said Marcia. "I remember when Bill was little he fell off the jungle gym and broke his arm in five places. The poor little guy was in such pain. It was awful to watch him. I couldn't keep him from hurting, but at least I could be there to comfort him and dry his tears. On the way to the emergency room, we prayed together that God would help him to be brave while the doctor fixed his arm.

"Now I am 'on his back' if I say anything about his drinking. He doesn't see alcohol as the source of his troubles at all. It's just a 'symptom,' he says, of all the things that have gone wrong in his life. When be broke his arm we didn't worry about why he'd fallen from the jungle gym, we just thought about getting him to the emergency

room and easing his pain. And in those days, he trusted me
and the doctor and everyone who loved him to help him
stop hurting."

I understand how this woman felt. Harry and I
agonized as we watched our sons become more entangled
in the snare of the disease that we knew so well. If we'd
seen one of them limping around with some physical
injury, we could have offered our sympathy and advice.
Would he have answered, "Leave me alone. I don't want to
hear about it! I like hopping around on one foot"? Probably
not. Alcoholism is not like a sprained ankle or a broken
bone.

Most parents will try to do *something* about a son's or
daughter's alcoholism. We tried sharing our own experiences, hoping that would be a warning and a deterrent.
But we should have known better. Eventually we realized
we couldn't do anything to control our adult children, nor
did we have the right to try. Al-Anon, a support group for
the family of the alcoholic, tells us:

> You can help only by facing up to these facts: he
> cannot control his drinking; you cannot force him to
> stop drinking by nagging, scolding, kindness or un-
> kindness. You will need to realize and admit that you
> have no more right to criticize, admonish, or demand
> sobriety of this adult than if he were a stranger. You
> can help him best if you can persuade yourself to Let
> Go—and Let God.[3]

LEARNING TO LET GO

That's good advice, but it's hard to take. A friend of
mine whose son is in jail because of drinking tells me that
she has had to discipline herself to release her son with

love. "The best thing I can offer him," she says, "is my whole, healthy self." She is right. It is too easy for us to get caught up in the disease of alcoholism and become emotionally ill ourselves.

Many of us do that. We let our child's alcoholism become the focal point of our lives. We become addicted to his addiction. If there are other children in the home, the disease can permeate the whole family. Even if there are not, it can erode the marriage relationship. Maybe that's where you are today. If so, you will identify with these words from an author who has walked in your footsteps. Her pamphlet "Parents in Crisis—Parents in Pain" is distributed to high school parents of troubled teens.

We are in PAIN. Somehow our children have slipped through our guiding fingers into danger. They dance on the razor's edge laughing, while we demand, threaten, and beg them to think. Each morning we pledge to try harder. Each night we collapse from fighting with our teens and our spouses. Sinking in anger, guilt and helplessness, we feel that our out-of-bounds adolescents have poked a hole in us. Our life is draining out. We are in CRISIS. What shall we do?

1. **Be honest.** Take the lid off the problem and take a look. We use a lot of energy denying and covering up our problems. We need that energy to examine our problems realistically.
2. **Let our son or daughter know We will survive.** They need to know we are strong.

3. **Keep our marriage a priority.** A rebelling teen stresses family relationships, especially between Mom and Dad.
4. **Take time to enjoy our other children.** They need normal loving interaction within the family. We need it, too.
5. **Focus on our own growth and change.** Just as the teen must change himself, we must change ourselves.
6. **Allow ourselves the freedom to enjoy life and to laugh.** Even if we have an area of painful concern, we can still have joy.
7. **Get help.** Reach out to the resources available. We need to search for support and information.[4]

A strong family will increase the chances of our young person's recovery from his addiction. We can tighten our family structure without shutting him out. Our love will provide the gate for his reentry into the security of our family circle—when *he* is ready.

If he is an adolescent, he may not be a true alcoholic. The teenage years are a time of transition. Teens "try on" many behavior patterns on their way to maturity. For us to detach ourselves emotionally from his problem of alcohol abuse is not to give up on him. We can love and encourage him, we can learn the facts about the nature of addiction, and we can be ready for action at a time when *doing* something will be productive.

Every natural instinct makes us want to rescue our child from disaster, but our task is to help him grow into the person God intended him to be. He is fumbling his way toward maturity, trying to answer the age-old question, "Who am I?" To release him with love is to:

- Allow him to learn from the consequences of his mistakes.
- Support him, not carry him.
- Care about him, not care for him.
- Change our responses and reactions, not try to change him.
- Love him for what he is, not what he does.
- Build him up, not tear him down.
- Talk to him, not at him.
- Hope for the best, not dwell on the worst.
- Live in love, not in fear.[5]

TOUGH LOVE

Phil M. spoke before a meeting of parents whose children were abusing alcohol and drugs. "We tried everything the experts told us to do before we gave up with Troy," he said. "The 'tough love' idea is great, but I finally came to a place where I couldn't stand the sight of him. 'Love' had gotten buried in the anger and frustration I felt over what Troy was doing to our family. Maggie, my wife, was an emotional wreck from all the stress, and neither of us had time for our other kids. I couldn't see my whole family sacrificed to Troy's addiction—sickness or not.

"We finally gave him an ultimatum, although Maggie thought we should give him one more chance. He'd had enough chances, as far as I was concerned. Anyway, I told him he had two choices. He could either go into a treatment center or he could pack his bags and get out. He was only seventeen, so he would have ended up a ward of the state and gone into some group home, if he didn't land in jail first. He didn't like it, but he went for treatment. And I *think* he's been sober ever since. It's hard to be sure because the level of trust between us is still so low. I told him if I caught him with so much as one beer, that was it. Maggie thinks I'm hard on him, but really, all I want to do is save his life. Isn't that love?"

"We couldn't get a treatment center to admit Andrea without her being willing to go," said another woman. "The recovery centers within our area told us that their program wouldn't be effective without her total cooperation. I think we were in denial that she had a *real* problem, anyway, so maybe that's what we wanted to hear. We sweated out her high school years, and then she moved into an apartment with a girlfriend. It was easier then, in a way, because we didn't have to wonder where she was and what she was doing every minute. But when we did see her, we felt more helpless than ever. Finally she went to AA on her own, and she's like a different person now."

"What *shouldn't* we do?"

Probably the most common role for the parent of an alcoholic to play is that of *Enabler*, a fitting term for one who unintentionally makes it easy for the alcoholic to continue drinking. According to Sharon Wegscheider, who sees each member of the alcoholic family in a different role: Dependent, Enabler, Scapegoat, etc., it is the person emotionally closest to the alcoholic who becomes the Enabler. Parents—mothers in particular—exhibit the classic symptoms of enabling when they

- *Deny* that there is a problem, making excuses and explanations for embarrassing episodes, thereby reinforcing the alcoholic child's denial.
- *Conceal* from other family members and friends dented fenders, lost jobs, and other unpleasant results of a drinking bout.

- *Protect* their alcoholic child from the inevitable consequences of his alcoholism, calling school or work with explanations for his absence, replacing lost or squandered money, doing his chores for him. Eventually they
- *Take over* many of his responsibilities, making it possible for him to go on drinking.

This pattern of denial, concealment, protection, and taking-over is the understandable extension of a parent's natural desire to care for and protect his child. Only when a parent is convinced that such behavior is acting against his child's best interest can he be persuaded to withdraw his well-intentioned efforts.

"I look back in amazement at the way my parents reacted to my drinking," said twenty-four-year-old Shawn. "An uncle had the gall to mention the word 'alcoholism' and my dad hit the roof. 'Not my son!' he bellowed. The uncle is an alcoholic himself, so he knew the signs. My folks lectured me about self-control and pleaded with me to cut down, combed my room and searched my car for hidden bottles. Finally they paid the rent on an apartment so they could kick me out, gently! My dad even found me a job and gave me his old car. But they wouldn't believe I was an alcoholic until I landed in the hospital."

A NEED TO BE NEEDED

There are subtle payoffs for the parent-enabler. Most of us experience some degree of loss as our children outgrow their need for our care and guidance. As our children gradually mature into responsible adults, our pride in them and the satisfaction of having fulfilled our responsibility as parents compensate for this loss. When alcohol enters the picture during the growing-up process, maturing is interrupted. Instead of the gradual development of independence in the child, there is his sudden demand to be left alone. He tolerates no interference in his pursuit of the next drink. He has found the solution to every problem. Alcohol is his panacea. He no longer brings his growing pains for our parental soothing. We are bewildered and hurt. We're not ready to let go, especially when we see that our child is not ready to be independent.

An alcoholic wants neither advice nor guidance. But he could use some sympathy now and then for the "bad breaks" he seems to be getting. And he'd be grateful for a loan to tide him over until payday. And would we mind calling the boss to tell him he has a touch of the flu this morning and can't make it in? If this kind of help is the only kind he wants from us, we'll give it. We can't abandon our own child, can we? Where would he be without us?

"That's just how my mother felt," said Shawn. "She was the last to let go. I ended up on the street because my dad refused to keep paying my rent, and I didn't have enough money to buy food. I couldn't believe that Mom wouldn't send me a lousy twenty bucks—that she'd let me go hungry! I know now that it almost destroyed her to say no. But when I found myself standing in the soup line at the rescue mission, hoping I could get a bed in the armory for the night—they let us in when the temperature got below forty degrees, women and children first, single men last—something happened inside of me.

"I think God let me see myself as I really was, a bum among bums. But at the same time I felt His love. And if there was something there for Him to love, that 'something' could be my strength. That was when I began to get well."

A MOTHER'S PRAYER

Shawn's parents praise God for their son's recovery. "We finally came to a place where we had to admit defeat," his mother said. "We'd tried everything in our power, and nothing had worked. Our entire concentration had been on Shawn's drinking, and our marriage was coming apart. One morning I came upon a verse in James: 'And the prayer offered in faith will make the sick person well; the Lord will raise him up. If he has sinned, he will be forgiven' (James 5:15).

"I felt the Lord was speaking right to me. That's it, I thought. I can't make him well, but prayer can. I can't raise him up, but the Lord will. My only part is the 'prayer offered in faith.' I prayed that morning with all the faith I could muster, asking the Lord to heal Shawn. An hour later he telephoned to ask for money, and for the first time I was able to say no."

One parent after another shares a story of trial and error, of doing too much in desperation or nothing at all in ignorance. As we made mistakes with our toddlers, we'll continue to do so with our teens and adult children. We must remember that our parenting, past or present, is not the cause of our child's addiction. Alcoholism is a disease, as real as diabetes, but one that the alcoholic himself must acknowledge before he will begin to recover.

A BATTLE GROUND

My friend Barbra and I share the heartache of parents whose children have been crippled by alcoholism. Her son and mine are victims of this sickness of body and spirit. We are like the mothers of young men who have gone to war. Our children are engaged in a battle where the enemy is alcohol, and we can only wait and pray for their victory and safe return. We imagine our sons in the front lines and see them struck down, mortally wounded by their adversary. At the very least, we think, they will emerge from the war with emotional scars that may never heal.

We are tempted to despair. But it is our service to discipline our minds and control our images. We know that the Lord to whom we pray is beside our sons, ready to lead them out of the battle zone. Our prayer for their protection and our peace of mind is expressed in Paul's words to the Ephesians:

> Finally, be strong in the Lord and in his mighty power. Put on the full armor of God so that you can take your stand against the devil's schemes. For our struggle is not against flesh and blood, but against the rulers, against the authorities, against the powers of this dark world and against the spiritual forces of evil in the heavenly realms. Therefore put on the full armor of God, so that when the day of evil comes, you may be able to stand your ground, and after you have done everything, to stand.
>
> *(Eph. 6:10–13)*

SUMMARY

- Parents are not to blame for their child's alcoholism.
- Our culture encourages and endorses the use of alcohol.
- By age eighteen, a child will have seen 100,000 beer commercials.
- Early signs of alcoholism may be mistaken for adolescent behavior.
- Parents cannot control their child's drinking by nagging, scolding, kindness, or unkindness.
- Parents need education and support from others who have walked in their shoes.

"How Can You Do This To Me?"

A television commercial for alcohol and drug treatment centers shows a wrecking ball slamming into a house—the kind of picturesque little home you see on a tree-shaded street in the suburbs, with picket fence and manicured lawn and a basketball hoop over the driveway for the kids. An inside shot shows a cozy room with easy chairs drawn invitingly to the hearth and family portraits on the mantle. Then suddenly the swinging ball breaks through, and the wall explodes into splinters and collapses in a rain of debris. Books and bric-a-brac topple from the shelves, the portraits tilt and crash to the bricks below. The camera closes in on still smiling faces, obscured now by the shattered glass within their twisted frames. This metaphor stabs at me, stripping away the comforting veneer of intervening years and uncovering painful memories of a dying marriage.

It didn't happen for me—nor does it for others—with the swift finality of a wrecking ball hitting a building. A family disintegrates gradually from the foundation up, beginning with the tiniest crack in the marriage bond. In an imperfect world of fallible human beings, most of us acquire a few cracks in the foundations of our marriages. We are all vulnerable, and every marriage has its special weaknesses. But when alcoholism invades a marriage, it dissolves relationships just as surely as the wrecking ball smashes glass and plaster. Hairline cracks of misunderstanding widen into chasms of resentment. What begins as an alliance of love between two people deteriorates into cold war or open conflict. As the family's foundation—the marital bond—weakens and collapses, the family itself is destroyed.

"What comes first, the alcohol problem or the bad marriage?"

You're wondering if the alcoholic is driven to drink by his unhappy marriage. Maybe it's your own marriage you're thinking of and you wonder what you've been doing wrong. If so, you can lay down your burden of guilt. You are no more to blame for your partner's alcohol addiction than for her PMS or his hay fever.

Many—probably most—of us have had unhappy marriages. But as sober alcoholics, if we have arrived at some degree of self-honesty, we've learned better than to blame our alcoholism on our circumstances. With hindsight, we can no longer blame bad marriages, lousy jobs, rebellious kids, noisy neighbors, or inclement weather. The stress of a miserable marriage may well accelerate the alcoholic's disease, but the stress is probably the result rather than the cause of the alcoholic behavior.

The best of marriages have their times of discontent. A good marriage survives those times and grows stronger as differences are resolved. An unhappy marriage develops when these differences are unresolved. Marriage "repair and maintenance"—mending those inevitable cracks in the marital foundation—is hard and humbling work. Most of us are driven to this maintenance work when the discomfort of marital tension outweighs the dread of head-on confrontation.

"For me, it was so much easier to let resentments silently build than to risk open warfare with Jack," said Jenny, a recovering alcoholic. "I grew up in a dysfunctional family where I spent my childhood trying to escape the constant bickering and arguing between my parents. There was never any 'talking things out' between them—just accusations and recriminations and bitterness. I didn't want my own marriage to be like that."

COPING WITH CONFLICT

Jenny chose to avoid marital conflict and learned to relieve her tension with alcohol. After years of sobriety, she looks back on the dynamics of her failed marriage and explains how her drinking affected it:

"It's taken me these ten years since my divorce to understand what happened between Jack and me when I was drinking," Jenny began. "We struggled from the start, mostly because I was so immature and sensitive. He *was* hard to live with—ambitious, hard-working, too demanding of himself and me. I had three babies, one after another. (And I say *I* had them, because it seemed like the responsibility for them was all mine. Jack didn't have time or the inclination to help.) He worked nights, moonlighting, while he was trying to get his law practice going, and I was stir-crazy from being home alone so much.

"We had one car in those days, and if I waited until

Saturday to do the grocery shopping and other errands, Jack would insist I take the children with me, so he could concentrate on the work he brought home. It was such a hassle that I began to order groceries by phone and have them delivered. I can't remember when I started ordering the bottle of sherry along with the peanut butter and baby food.

"My glass of wine was like a reward to myself after a hard day. I'd put the children to bed first and then sit down with my sherry while I read the paper and got a second wind. I always wanted to have the house spruced up before Jack got home, so he wouldn't pick at me about jam on the doorknob or toys in the hallway or something. He was such a perfectionist. He thought the house should always look as tidy as the day we bought it, even with three pre-schoolers. So I'd have my private "happy hour" and then run around getting things in order, ready to greet Jack with a smile on my face.

"At first Jack seemed to enjoy my new relaxed attitude when he came home, and sometimes we would have a glass of wine together. It seemed to relieve the tension he always brought home with him, and we could talk to each other like we used to when we were dating. He'd tell me about his hard day at the office, and I could listen and be sympathetic. Of course it worked both ways, and he was willing to hear about my problems. We'd encourage each other and be feeling really close and mellow by the time we went to bed. I think that was the best period of our whole marriage.

"But after a while I started sampling the sherry before I put the kids to bed, and I was more and more relaxed when Jack came home. I got so relaxed that I stopped worrying about the clutter he hated, and I felt hurt and misunderstood when he reverted to his old critical ways. But instead of flaring up at him or getting on the defensive, I'd just pour myself another drink to take the edge off my hurt. Rather than risk an unsympathetic response, I kept my wounded feelings to myself.

"In the beginning the alcohol had 'oiled my tongue,' as they say, and given me the courage to express myself to Jack in what might have been a healthy way. As time went on, though, drinking became such an outlet in itself that my *need* to talk diminished. I guess I didn't listen very well either because Jack had less and less to say. Instead of joining me for a drink when he came home, he'd just grumble his way to bed. It happened little by little, but my drinking changed our relationship forever."

COMMUNICATION PROBLEMS

Alcohol has a profound effect upon the communication between people. It has been correctly described as a "social lubricant," and many people experience the cocktail party phenomenon where a drink or two will transform total strangers into soulmates. But a husband and wife are not strangers at a cocktail party who can lay aside inhibitions just long enough for conversational intimacy. Marriage is the ultimate intimacy. Layers of disappointment, misunderstanding, and resentment will arise in the post-honeymoon world to cloud the developing bond. If these layers are resolved with honest communication as they arise, the foundation of the marriage is reinforced with the couple's growing understanding of each other. Feelings of hurt and anger that are ignored or buried or swallowed (with a chaser of alcohol) will seek another avenue of expression.

"I see now that drinking was my way of avoiding

issues and quieting my own inner turmoil," Jenny continued. "If I thought about it at all, I thought it was helping my relationship with Jack, but I was buying peace at too high a price. We did have a lot of differences, and maybe we wouldn't have made it together anyway, but if I'd had the courage to endure our inevitable clashes, we might have gradually come to understand each other. We did start out by falling in love, after all. I guess I thought the honeymoon should last forever."

Good marriages are held together by commitment, communication, and compassion. Commitment was there in the beginning of Jenny and Jack's marriage, but it needed the other elements to stay alive. Communication, good and/or bad, is the lifeblood of every marriage bond and will ultimately either strengthen or destroy it. Compassion is a natural result of effective communication between partners.

Unhappy marriages are not *lacking* in communication, for we continuously communicate with each other, by our actions if not our words. We send messages to each other at every turn. We convey tenderness by an affectionate pat, anger in a withering glance, understanding in a small act of consideration.

Jenny's earlier attempts at neatness were an unspoken message to Jack. The message said that she cared enough about him to honor his desire for an orderly place to come home to. Although she was tired at the end of the day and the clutter didn't bother her, she was willing to put Jack's needs ahead of her own. Jack responded as much to Jenny's efforts to please him as he did to the neat surroundings that he enjoyed. Jenny's unspoken statement and Jack's response set the scene for relaxed verbal communication between them. As they shared the events of their days and their feelings about what was happening in their life together, understanding and compassion began to grow.

A TWO-FACED COIN

As Jenny explained, in the beginning alcohol seemed to be a positive element in her relationship with Jack. Although alcohol is in fact a depressant, it acted initially like a stimulant, enabling Jenny to expend a little more energy than she seemed to be able to muster in her natural fatigue. Because alcohol is an anesthetic, a glass of wine relaxed the tension she felt as she waited for Jack in the evening, apprehensive about what she might have left undone.

Jenny was a woman programmed for alcoholism, both by temperament and by circumstances. Alcohol seemed to answer a very real need at a time in her life when she was vulnerable and immature. Because she was also physiologically set up for addiction, it took more and more alcohol for her to achieve the effect that she had experienced in the beginning.

"I kept trying to recapture those times when I'd felt relaxed and close to Jack. One drink, I thought, would do us both good. I'd just have one drink this time, two at the most. But no matter how I tried to limit or space my drinks, I seemed to go from tensely sober to out-of-control drunk.

"I didn't drink during the daytime, but by late afternoon every nerve in my body was rigid and screaming for that first glass of wine. As the time for Jack to come home approached, I began to panic, and the more anxious I felt, the more I drank. Any possibility of constructive communication between us was dissolved in alcohol before he drove in the driveway.

"To Jack's credit, he did everything he knew to save our deteriorating marriage," Jenny continued. "As my drinking increased, he could feel that I was withdrawing emotionally from him. When he tried to talk to me, all I could hear was his criticism, and I just went further into my shell. He was disappointed, I know, in me *and* my slipshod housekeeping, but in his way he did love me. He swallowed his pride and went to talk to our pastor, but that good-hearted man knew nothing about alcoholism, and his advice to Jack was less than helpful.

"They decided between them that my problem was a spiritual one that I could conquer by repentance and prayer. They didn't know that I'd repented and prayed over and over again. The thing was, I was asking God to help me *control* my drinking. I didn't know—or wouldn't face the fact—that control was not an option for me. When my prayers went unanswered, I thought that God had abandoned me. I couldn't blame Him. I hated myself. How could He love me? Actually, God was answering my prayers by bringing me to a point of desperation."

"Wouldn't she stop if she loved me?"

Jack asked himself that question as he watched Jenny's alcoholism destroy their marriage and family life. He knew he hadn't been easy to live with and he suspected that he was the real cause for Jenny's drinking, that he had not measured up to what she expected in a husband.

"I've always been too wrapped up in my business," he told their pastor. "I guess I took our marriage for granted. I love Jenny, but I've never been able to be very demonstrative or affectionate. And it's been a long time since she's shown any affection toward me. She probably married me more to get away from home than because she loved me. I'm not such a lovable guy anyway. If she loved me, she wouldn't keep on drinking while our marriage goes down the drain."

Alcoholics drink because of their addiction, not because of a lack of love. Jenny was the victim of disease, and a disease is a condition, not an act. Like other alcoholics, she had lost her ability to choose whether she would drink or not. Unfortunately, the love between Jenny and Jack failed to survive their battle with alcohol and they were eventually divorced.

"I'd been sober for over a year when Jack and I separated," Jenny said, "but we just couldn't seem to repair the damage that had been done. Until I found a program that helped restore me to sanity, I had a hard time coping with reality. So much garbage had accumulated between us. We both tried, but we kept stumbling over old resentments and piling on new ones. I hung on to my sobriety an hour at a time, at first, and if Jack so much as looked at me the wrong way or used the wrong tone of voice, I'd fall apart."

Most recovering alcoholics can identify with Jenny's emotional instability during the first months of her sobriety. She needed as much TLC as if she'd been recovering from any other illness, and Jack needed time to recover from the anger and bitterness Jenny's drinking had caused him. They were unable to fulfill each other's needs in the beginning of Jenny's recovery.

"Why am I not enough for him?"

Most husbands or wives of alcoholics suffer the agony of self-doubt, feeling that they are not *doing* enough or *being* enough for their drinking spouses. As the addiction progresses and the alcoholic becomes more adept at denial of his illness, he is likely to compound his partner's undeserved guilt with accusations: "If you'd get off my back I wouldn't drink so much." Or, "If you'd have dinner ready when I come home, . . ." Or, "If you wouldn't run up the phone bill, . . ." Or, "If you'd fix yourself up once in a while like other women, . . ." He is desperately trying to justify his drinking, to find valid reasons to hang on to the alcohol that he cannot bear to give up.

"I could always find reasons for that first drink of a binge," said Dwight. "Well, who couldn't? If a fouled-up, aggravating day at work wasn't enough to justify buying that first six-pack of beer on the way home, I'd pick a fight with Marge and use her lack of understanding and rotten disposition as my rationale. When I finally got to AA, they told me that it was my body screaming for a fix that tricked my mind into paving the way for another binge. They told me that I would always find a reason but never an excuse. Alcohol is cunning, baffling, and powerful. It dulls the mind, warps the personality, and tears marriages apart. It almost finished mine."

A PERFECT MISTRESS

"I thought I was going crazy," Marge said. "Dwight had me convinced that I was a primary cause for his drinking, and I was tiptoeing around trying to keep the home front peaceful and comfortable for him, so he wouldn't *have* to go out and drink again. But I always fell short of *his* expectations, and off he'd go. Sometimes he'd slam out of the house in the middle of dinner and sometimes he'd just quietly disappear while I was putting

the kids to bed. I finally decided he was having an affair
and covering his guilt by getting drunk."

Marge's suspicion was understandable. Many wives of
alcoholics have felt the same. As a man's relationship with
his wife deteriorates, his alcohol becomes more important
than ever. He has found his ideal, nonthreatening relationship in his affair with the bottle. Alcohol is both friend
and lover, ever faithful to soothe wounded feelings when
life seems harsh.

Like the unfaithful husband, he knows that tonight's
pursuit of pleasure will create more dissension at home
tomorrow, but the immediate reward seems worth it. He
needs an escape from today's misery. He closes his eyes to
the inevitable long-term consequences of his behavior in
his search for short-term gratification. It's a poor trade-off,
but a classic symptom of addiction.

Although Dwight had not become involved with a
flesh and blood mistress, he had transferred his allegiance
from his wife and family to his alcohol. The effect on his
marriage was just as devastating.

"Can't she see what she's doing to the family?"

Alcoholics are notorious for their nearsightedness.
Life beyond themselves and their misery is out of focus.
Their common perspective is one of denial, for to see
alcohol as a problem is to face the unfaceable. If the
alcoholic has any awareness of the suffering his loved ones
are experiencing, he must find reasons other than his
drinking for their pain. He will go to any lengths to
rationalize and justify his own contribution to the family
turmoil.

Kent accuses Carol of keeping their lives in a constant
state of emergency with her unreliability and inconsis-

tency. "I can't depend on her to pick Rob up at Cub Scouts or get Heidi to the orthodontist on time for her appointment," he complains. "I always seem to be going behind her and picking up the pieces of her broken promises. Her problem is that she's just plain selfish and immature."

Carol protests that she has too much to do, that too much is expected of her, that her mother-in-law is driving her crazy, that Kent doesn't appreciate her efforts to keep the household running smoothly. Denial. Kent sees Carol's drinking as just one character flaw among many. Also denial. Neither wants to face the possibility of alcoholism in their family.

DAVE'S STORY

My husband and I had breakfast with a new friend, happily remarried after his 33-year marriage to an alcoholic woman had ended in divorce.

"I stayed in my first marriage far too long," Dave told us, "but I kept thinking I could fix it, that if I just handled things the right way that Lil would have to stop drinking and then our family could live a normal life. And, believe me, I was determined to handle it. I wouldn't have asked some outsider for help on a bet. What kind of man can't control his own wife? I didn't want to let anyone in on what was happening in our house.

"Once our family doctor suspected that Lil was drinking too much and asked me about it. I opened up a little bit to him, but as soon as he mentioned Alcoholics Anonymous, I was furious. How dared he think my wife was an alcoholic! I was mortified that our problems might show to the outside world, and I was more determined than ever to stop her boozing. I was head of the house and she was obligated to do what I demanded.

"She didn't drive and I did the grocery shopping, so I tried sabotaging her drinking by 'forgetting' to buy the booze she ordered. But it didn't work. She'd find a way to get more while I was at work. I'd come home and she'd be standing at the sink with a glass in her hand. 'Are you drinking?' I'd ask. 'Of course not,' she'd say. 'This is water. Why are you so suspicious?' Then she'd refuse to kiss me because she said I was just checking up on her and wanted to smell her breath. I was never really sure whether she was telling the truth or not. Anyway, we'd sit down to dinner and I'd be feeling half guilty for accusing her. Then she'd start talking and slurring her words and I'd *know* she was drinking.

"Then all communication between us would stop and she'd drink openly until she passed out. I always had this ritual—I'd go out in the garage with a flashlight and start looking for evidence. I had two trashcans so I could transfer garbage from one can to another and count bottles that she'd buried under milk cartons and soup cans. It was insane. What was I going to do with this information when I got it? But somehow I had to know.

"At one point—you may find this hard to believe—I sold everything and moved the family to Denmark, thinking that the cost of living there was so high that there wouldn't be any room in the budget for liquor. We lived out of suitcases for six months while I found out that plan wouldn't work.

"You can imagine how this crazy lifestyle was for the kids. They'd ask, 'Mom, why do you drink so much?' and she'd say, "That's the only way I can live with kids like you and a loser like your father!' Even so, they were very protective of her. Of course, I did all the disciplining. I'd get a full report of their misdeeds when I got home at night and then I'd be expected to straighten them out. As a consequence, they blamed me for making their lives miserable. Two of them won't have anything to do with me today.

"The thing is I felt responsible underneath, because Lil wasn't an alcoholic when I married her. So something about me must have driven her to drink. And if I'd caused her to be a drunk, it was up to me to change her, I thought. But whatever I did, she just got worse.

"She must have felt hopeless herself, because she threatened suicide frequently. I'd come home to find her gone and a note on the table that she was sick of me and the kids and was going to end it all. I'd spend the next three days looking for her, calling police stations and hospitals, and then she'd show up again. 'Where have you been?' I'd ask, when I came home to find her sitting at the kitchen table as if nothing had happened. 'None of your business,' she'd answer.

"Someone asked me later if I didn't secretly wish she'd carry out her threat and end our misery once and for all. But I never felt that. Instead, I wanted to die myself. I thought about suicide more than once, but I knew my insurance policy wouldn't pay off if I killed myself, and I couldn't leave her without protection, even after the kids had grown up. I was at the end of my rope.

"I'd given up praying, because I figured that a God that really cared about me wouldn't let this happen to my life. I was an undeserving victim of circumstances with no power, I thought, to do anything about them. I'd given up on God, but I guess He hadn't given up on me. He finally cut through my pride and made me willing to get help. I found out in my Al-Anon group that I had become as sick as Lil over the years. That's when the healing began."

Dave's was the story of a sad marriage that failed to survive the damage caused by Lil's alcoholism. He survived with his healing years in Al-Anon and Lil eventually survived by finding sobriety. But it was too late for their marriage. The damage to their relationship was irreversible.

ANN'S STORY

Dave met and married Ann, a widow with five young children. Ann had been married for twenty years to Jake, a man whose broken life had ended in an alcoholic stupor. We'd known Jake and Ann since the early years of their marriage and had watched the deterioration of their home and family as Jake's drinking had gone from occasional partying to daily dependence. His personality had changed over the years until the friendly, gentle young man we'd once known had become a sullen, ill-humored stranger.

"I was raised to believe that the fulfillment of my life—any woman's life—would be found in my role as wife and mother," Ann told us. "My disappointment in marriage was devastating. I was in labor with our second baby when Jake escaped into a weekend binge the first time, and after that it was all downhill. He couldn't face any of the responsibilities of caring for a family, and I gradually took over every chore. He had a couple of brief periods of sobriety when everyone walked on eggs for fear we'd say or do something to set him off again, but there was no way we could avoid doing *something* wrong. Randy and the twins were conceived during those sober intervals."

I remembered Ann in those days, always smiling even when I knew that her home life was a nightmare.

"Well, in a way I *was* happy," she explained. "The children were my heart's delight, and I was constantly seeking God's will about Jake. I wanted him to be happy, and I figured it was up to me to make him happy by creating a normal home life. I wanted for him what I wanted for myself—just to find fulfillment and happiness within our family. But he wouldn't or couldn't be satisfied with what we had, and I couldn't produce harmony by myself.

"There were some sad developments in the last years of our life together. At one point Jake had what I believe was a truly spiritual experience where he saw Jesus and heard a message from God. God told him that he should run. Not run away, but run and jog for exercise. The counselor confirmed this when he explained that alcoholics don't seem to produce endorphins—chemicals in the brain that give us a natural "high"—and that strenuous exercise could activate and stimulate that production. Well, Jake started an exercise program and got sober and off of drugs, but it didn't last.

"About that time it came out in counseling that he'd been sexually molested by his grandfather as a child, and he just couldn't handle it. He'd buried those memories for so long and when they surfaced, he just went berserk emotionally. He didn't have stable enough sobriety to deal with his pain, so he started to drink and use again for the last time. By the time he was dying there was no marriage left, and the man in the hospital ward bore no resemblance to the Jake I'd married."

As Ann talked I was remembering a bright young couple proudly posing with their first baby at his baptism. A grinning Jake wrapped his long arms around Ann and their tiny son as if to shield his family from any danger that might lurk beyond the security of their home. He was a happy man. Life was sweet.

In twenty years, their life was robbed of sweetness: the man, dead of alcoholism; the woman, a survivor smiling through her scars; the infant, a nineteen-year-old street person spaced out on drugs. Jake had been ready to guard his treasure from outside threats, but he'd failed to see the danger—for him—in a cup of sparkling punch at the baptismal celebration. Our Lord's words could apply to a marriage ravaged by addiction to alcohol:

> But understand this: if the owner of the house had known at what hour the thief was coming, he would not have let his house be broken into.
>
> *(Luke 12:39)*

DESTRUCTION FROM WITHIN

I read a news article about the sugar maples of Vermont—those spectacular beauties whose autumn colors quicken the pulse and whose sap provides a leading industry for that New England state. Every year when the snows melt, the sap rises ready to be tapped, dripping into old-fashioned buckets or modern tubing to begin its journey to your breakfast table and mine. Is there anything more delicious than a crisp waffle or fluffy pancake swimming in a pool of real maple syrup?

But there's trouble at the source of our gastronomical pleasure. The pear thrip, a tiny insect smaller than a flea, has invaded the maple forests. They drill holes in the tender maple buds and suck out the vital juices. Leaves drop and trees die, robbed from within of their energy. The enemy, invisible to the unwary eye, rages within.

Jake and Ann's marriage was like the sugar maple, beautiful to behold, standing firm against the onslaught of rain and wind. The thrip in their lives was alcoholism. Their story is repeated again and again in families across the nation. Alcoholic marriages don't collapse suddenly like the house in the path of the wrecking ball. Alcoholism invades a marriage as the thrip invades the maple forest, causing it to disintegrate slowly from within. The vital juices of the marital relationship—trust, respect, communication—are sucked dry by the insidious disease of alcoholism.

The damage to an alcoholic marriage need not be permanent nor irreversible. Hope lies in the awareness that comes with understanding the disease. Education can help the bewildered spouse of an alcoholic to identify the thief of his marital joy and take a stand against the enemy. Marriages as well as individuals can survive and overcome the blight of alcoholism. With effective help, the dark days can serve as a background for renewal. The bright promise that once surrounded the couple as they spoke their wedding vows can be restored.

SUMMARY

- Husbands or wives are not to blame for their partner's alcoholism.

- Alcohol may appear to improve communication between spouses.

- Alcoholism ultimately destroys communication in marriage.

- Alcoholic behavior makes for an unhappy marriage.

- Although the alcoholic may blame his drinking on conflict in his marriage, the conflict is probably the result, not the cause, of his drinking.

- Alcoholics drink because of their addiction, not because of a lack of love.

- Alcohol is to the alcoholic as a mistress is to an unfaithful husband.

- The alcoholic is blind to what is happening to his marriage.

- With education and effective help, there is hope for restoration and renewal of the alcoholic marriage.

"Is Daddy Home Yet?"

"Today is the day!" Eric shouted across the playground to his brother Brian as the final bell rang at Parkview Elementary. "Dad's taking us to the carnival this afternoon!" Eric broadjumped across a puddle on the lawn and swung his lunchpail high as the two boys met and made their way toward the yellow school bus. "Aren't you excited, Bry?"

"Yeah, sure," the older boy answered. "But don't count on it, okay?"

Brian stared out the window of the bus, remembering the events of the past week. Their dad had made a big deal over the carnival on Sunday, about how it would be a special outing for just the guys and how they'd have corn dogs and cotton candy and how they'd try for one of those prizes at the bottle-toss booth—something to bring home to Mom. "One day this week, for sure," he'd said. "We'll have a blast." Dad was in a good mood Sunday, laughing and rumpling Eric's blond hair and throwing fake punches at Brian.

When Eric brought it up again Wednesday at dinner, Dad said he didn't want to be bugged about it. "I promised you, didn't I?" he snapped. "We'll go first chance we get. Now don't keep hounding me." Their Mom got that look on her face like she had when Eric slammed the door on his finger or when Brian cut his chin and had to have stitches. Eric wondered if Dad knew it was the last week the carnival would be in town, but he was afraid to bring it up again. He asked Brian and Brian asked Mom. Later they heard Mom talking in a low voice to Dad about not disappointing the boys with empty promises. Brian wouldn't be disappointed much because he knew better than to take Dad seriously in the first place, but Eric was just a little kid and he really got excited about things like carnivals. Anyway, Dad had come into their room this morning and said they would absolutely, positively go this afternoon. Brian was beginning to think that maybe it would be kind of fun after all. He had some birthday money saved.

Eleanor, Eric and Brian's mother, folded laundry with one eye on the kitchen clock. Clark left work at two o'clock on Fridays, so he should be home before the bus delivered the boys from school. He should be coming in the door any minute now, if he hadn't stopped at the Maverick for a couple of beers, as he and his buddies often did on Friday afternoons. Actually, Clark *always* stopped there when the work week was over, except for those times when he'd sworn off drinking forever and stayed on the wagon for a few weeks. But surely he wouldn't stop today when he knew the boys would be waiting for him.

Her throat tightened as she remembered Eric's tears

and the hurt in Brian's eyes the last time Clark had "forgotten" an appointment with his sons. They'd planned a picnic supper on the beach, and the boys had made brownies and helped pack the fried chicken and potato salad in the wicker hamper, so they'd be all set for the short drive to the lake when Clark came home. They'd waited two hours, playing Old Maid to pass the time, and then they'd unpacked the food and eaten their cold supper at the kitchen table. Eric said Dad must have had a flat tire or something. Brian put his fist down hard on the package of brownies, smashing most of them, and went to his room. Eleanor swore that night that she'd learn to drive and buy a little used car, so they wouldn't be so dependent on Clark. Of course she didn't follow through. It was just another one of her fantasies.

A REPEAT PERFORMANCE

Now it was happening again: Eric running the block from the bus stop, bursting in the door, face flushed and eyes bright with anticipation of an evening with Dad at the carnival. Brian nonchalantly taking his books to his room, then shaking the coins out of his piggy bank, just in case.

By four o'clock Eleanor knew that Clark wasn't coming. Brian changed his clothes and went out to shoot baskets with his friend next door. Eric stayed by the dining room window, waiting and watching the cars turn into the cul de sac. There was still time, but he wished Dad would hurry or some of the carnival rides might close down. Eric stood at the window for a long time.

Clark arrived eventually, after the boys were in bed, walking carefully, as if the linoleum was moving beneath his feet like the funhouse floor at the carnival. Eleanor didn't need to look at him to know that he'd been at the

Maverick. She didn't feel like looking at him or listening to his clumsy excuses.

"It just couldn't be helped, Ellie. Mack's wife served him with divorce papers at the plant today, and he was practically suicidal. After all the times he's stood by me, there was no way I could leave him like that. He needed a drink bad. What was I supposed to do? I thought you'd understand if you knew the circumstances. Of course, I should have called, but I didn't dare leave him for a minute."

"Clark, the boys were waiting. You could have—"

"And do you know it actually started to rain as we were leaving work? There wouldn't have been much point in going to the carnival in the rain now, would there? That carnival will come around again. Anyway, Pete said he took his kids last week and it wasn't that good—probably would have been a big disappointment for Eric and Brian. I don't think Brian was that excited about it anyway. Don't you think he's been kind of sullen lately? I don't know what's wrong with that kid."

"I think I do, Clark," Eleanor sighed.

"What then? Me, I suppose. Boy, you sit there looking so glum and so superior. Miss Pureheart herself. How about that time you had too much wine and couldn't even get dinner on the table? Where's my dinner, by the way? I don't suppose anyone thought I might be hungry after all the stress of trying to keep my best friend from killing himself. No wonder I stop in for a beer now and then. Coming home to this family is like walking into a morgue. Oh, what the hell, I'm going to bed!"

Clark's words pierced the wall of Brian and Eric's bedroom, pierced and wounded the tender hearts of the two little boys. Brian pulled his pillow over his head, trying to shut out the angry sounds, but the ugly words kept echoing inside his head. He hoped Eric had slept through the racket, but he could tell from the way the bed creaked that his little brother was awake, probably curled into a ball around his stuffed rabbit like when he was a baby. Brian had tried to warn him. He should have told him that Dad might have something more important come up . . . more important than a dumb carnival.

Eric stared into the dark corners of the bedroom, rubbing the soft rabbit fur against his cheek and squeezing his eyes shut against the imaginary monsters that lived in the shadows. He knew they were imaginary, but they made him feel scared all the same. He wished Mom would come in and tuck him in again. He wished Dad wouldn't sound so mean, as if everything were Mom's fault. He heard a door slam and burrowed deeper into his covers.

Eric knew it was his fault that he'd talked about the carnival in the first place. That's what Dad and Mom were fighting about. He'd really wanted to go today, so much that his stomach was beginning to hurt when they were waiting for Dad to come. He shouldn't have kept talking about it. It was his fault.

SUFFER THE LITTLE CHILDREN

Scenes like these are played over and over again in homes across the country. Some of the estimated fifteen million children of alcoholics live nightmares of abuse and neglect. At best, they suffer from warped relationships with parents who withdraw from them one moment and smother them with affection the next.

There is a chance (alarmingly slim, according to statistics) that Clark will recognize his addiction, seek help, and begin to recover while his children are young enough to benefit from an improved home life. There is a greater chance that his disease of alcoholism will escalate and that the family will be stressed to the breaking point with relational conflicts, financial problems, and legal emergencies.

Even when the alcoholic parent becomes sober, the scars of the children remain. Most professionals agree with Anderson Spickard's statement: "No child of an alcoholic grows up undamaged. The damage can begin before birth and almost always casts a long shadow into adulthood."[1]

"Where is Daddy, anyway?"

I thought we were going on a picnic. He said he'd take us to the carnival. He promised to help with my Cub Scout project. I thought. . . . He said. . . . He promised. . . .

Eleanor had a variety of answers for her sons, concocted to soften the disappointment they experienced too often as they waited for their father to be where he said he would be. Something came up at work. He had trouble with the car. There was an emergency.

Inside, Eleanor fought the temptation to heap her own sorrow and frustration upon her small sons. Who else did she have to talk to or confide in? She couldn't tell her parents that Clark was drinking too much, that he'd rather spend his evenings at the Maverick with his friends than be with his wife and children. She almost told her sister Betsy once, but Betsy's husband was so perfect. He spent all his spare time with his family. Maybe Betsy and her kids were more fun to come home to. Maybe if she tried harder. . . .

"Listen, boys," she said one Saturday afternoon when Clark had gone to visit his brother. "Let's get the lawn mowed and the garage swept out and surprise Dad with a barbecue tonight. We'll all work together, and it will be fun. And please, fellows, don't start nagging at your father about the summer softball team the minute he comes home. You know how that upsets him. You can ask him after supper—if he's not too tired."

But it didn't work out. Clark called from Don's and said they'd decided to go and bowl a few games. He was sorry to disappoint them if they had something planned, but he had an obligation to his brother, too. Eleanor knew about the Saturday night gang at the bowling alley and the drinking that went on there. Clark and his brother Don had probably gotten a good start on the beer already. Their father had been a drunk, and it looked like they were following in his footsteps. Eleanor prayed that Eric and Brian would stay away from alcohol as they got older, or at least be strong enough to drink in moderation like her family. It was strange because Clark had seemed to have so much self-discipline when they got married.

"If it makes her sick, why does she drink that stuff?"

Thirteen-year-old Stacy Evans lived down the street from Clark and Eleanor and their little boys. Her brother Michael used to bring Brian home from school sometimes so they could play Captain Marvel in Michael's fort behind their house. They got on her nerves with their whooping and hollering, especially when her mother worked and she was babysitting, but it was better than the gloom that hung over their house these days. Mother had been laid off before Christmas and now, with the way she was, they couldn't bring anyone home.

"My dad explained it to Michael and me," Stacy confided to her friend Audrey. "Mother is sick. She has a disease called alcoholism and it's not her fault. It's like an allergy, you know. She's allergic to alcohol just like our cousin Jimmy is allergic to peanuts. Jimmy almost died from eating peanut butter when he was little, before anyone knew about the allergy. Promise you won't tell, though, because Daddy says it's private family business."

Stacy wanted Audrey to understand, but she had a hard time understanding herself. It seemed like Jimmy was smarter than her mother. After the time when he was so sick, you couldn't force him to eat anything with peanuts in it again. By the time he was three years old, he was telling everyone he couldn't eat peanuts. It was confusing. Stacy never could understand why Mother would drink the very stuff that made her sick. She didn't see how anyone could drink that junk anyway. The smell was enough to make you gag. Stacy was sure she'd never touch alcohol, not even champagne at her wedding.

SHARING THE PAIN

These are sad stories about sad youngsters. Our hearts ache for the innocent children in these alcoholic families. Unfortunately, our examples are mild in comparison to many of the stories told by adult children of alcoholics (ACAs). They sob out their stories from the psychiatrist's couch or in group sessions of other hurting ACAs or behind the closed door of the pastor's study, finally articulating their pain as they try to untangle the knots in their lives.

Debbie tells of terror-filled nights, crouching at the head of the stairs to listen to the thudding sounds and mewling cries that meant her mother would be withdrawn and silent for the days to come. It meant the long-sleeved blouse to hide the bruises. It meant being sent to the post office for the mail and to the corner store for groceries so that her mother could hide their secret from the world. It meant the rekindling of the hate she felt for her father and confusion because her love for him wouldn't quite go away.

Drew tells of being roused from sleep and prodded into the cold back seat of the old Chevy with his whimpering sister to be driven on dark and winding roads to his aunt's house.

"I'd be protesting that I was going to miss the school outing the next day, and my little sister would be crying and begging Mom to turn around and go home again. Mom and Dad were both alcoholics. They'd come home after work and start drinking. Sometimes they'd have a couple of Margaritas in the family room like I'd see some of my friends' parents doing and then we'd have dinner and act like a normal family. But other times they'd start arguing and keep on drinking while we made ourselves jellybread sandwiches and escaped to our rooms. Some nights they'd end up in a screaming fight and Mom would yank us out of bed and into the car to go to Aunt Dee's. I remember how cold that red plastic upholstery felt through my pajamas. I remember burying my head in the corner of the back seat rather than looking out at the dark canyons below as we flew around the curves. My mother was in no condition to drive on *any* road, and this one was a doozie. They used to say God watches out for fools and drunkards, and I guess it's true."

"I don't know which is worse, two battling parents or one who's missing altogether," said Gloria. "My father took off and left my mother with three little ones when I was just seven. He didn't say anything to us. Just left. Walked out. I remember a lot of confusing emotions. Guilt because maybe something I did made him leave. Fear

because Mother kept saying she "couldn't do it alone."
Embarrassment because our family didn't have a father
anymore and we were "different." Humiliation and anger
because I overheard someone saying that Daddy was a no-
good drunk. Mother did have a terrible struggle trying to
manage everything. She got county aid at first and then
went to work as a waitress after we were in school. It
seemed like she never could take us anywhere or come to
our school functions because she was either working the
dinner shift or too tired to go anywhere. I think I resented
her as much as my father. I thought she should be able to
figure out some way to make us a normal family.

"Daddy called home a couple of times when we were
teenagers, and we had this fantasy that he would come
back and make everything okay again, but he never did.
After he died, we found out from a relative that he'd been
too ashamed during his sober periods to face us. But it
would have been better for all of us if he had. Daddy's
leaving left a gap in my life, and for a long time I felt like I
wasn't a whole person. I felt that way until I came to know
Christ as Lord of my life and let God the Father fill that
emptiness in me."

A BLEAK FUTURE

Eric and Brian, Stacy and Michael, Debbie, Drew
and his sister, Gloria and her siblings—ten children
profoundly affected by their alcoholic parents. Out of
these ten, the statistics tell us that four will become
alcoholic adults. Children of alcoholics are four times
more likely than others to become problem drinkers.
According to some estimates, over 75 percent of the
children raised in an alcoholic family will either them-

selves develop a chemical dependency problem or marry an abuser.

The genetic factor combined with the personality problems that are apt to develop as a child grows up in a dysfunctional family almost guarantee the appearance of some kind of addiction or compulsion in adulthood.

"Why can't Mom make it better?"

Children look to the nonalcoholic parent to protect them and make their pain go away. Close friends and relatives, too, often wonder why the nonalcoholic spouse can't do more to counteract the damaging effects of the alcoholism. The truth is that the other, assumably more stable, partner becomes as emotionally ill as her drinking husband and is apt to do as much damage to the children as the alcoholic himself.

Eleanor fantasized about being less dependent upon Clark, but in reality she became more and more dependent upon him. In trying to protect her boys from the fact of their father's alcoholism, she deprived them of an answer to his neglect and verbal abuse. With her "let's keep Daddy happy" attitude, she implied that what Eric and Brian did or said might trigger a drinking bout or a bad scene. Her preoccupation with her alcoholic husband robbed her of time and energy that her sons desperately needed from her.

Stacy's father took a positive step in explaining to his children that alcoholism is a disease much like an allergy, but he was unable to counteract the gloomy atmosphere his wife's illness created in their home. His feelings of helplessness led him into a depression that compounded the family's problems. In telling Stacy and Michael that their mother's alcoholism was "private family business," he unintentionally transmitted his own feelings of embarrassment and shame caused by their situation.

Debbie's mother lived in a constant state of fear that her husband would come home drunk and turn his rage upon Debbie. On the nights that he was out drinking, she sent Debbie to her grandmother's for the night or upstairs early to do homework. She thought she was protecting her daughter by keeping her out of the way and taking the blows herself. With her own self-confidence destroyed by her husband's brutality, she was unaware of the emotional damage Debbie was sustaining.

Because both of Drew's parents were alcoholic, he and his sisters had a doubly hard time understanding what normal families were like. They had glimpses into the relative serenity of some of their friends' families, but their own role models were unable to give them the security they needed.

When her husband deserted her, Gloria's mother was overwhelmed with the sudden responsibility of three small children and the burden of being the sole provider for their physical needs. She had little emotional energy left over to meet their psychological needs or bring comfort to their wounded spirits.

Some wives or husbands of alcoholics involve their children actively in their fight against this bewildering disease. They enlist their aid in finding and throwing out hidden bottles or send them looking for the alcoholic parent at the neighborhood bar. The family becomes caught up in a series of crises, interspersed with short periods of hope. The nonalcoholic spouse, in his inability to cope with the snowballing effects of alcoholism on the family, passes on his feelings of anger, fear, and bitterness to his children.

A teenager decoded the secret message engraved on the hearts of all children of alcoholics when he said, "I don't know what's going on or who's fault it is or how to fight it. All I know is my Dad's booze is more important that I am."

Children of alcoholics have a difficult time finding their places within the family. Unable to develop healthy self-images, they take on roles that help them cope with circumstances beyond their understanding.

When my daughter Laurie was a pre-teen, she delighted in surprising me by cleaning up the kitchen or tidying up after her younger siblings. She left notes saying, "I love you, do you love me?" where I would find them. She tried to bring cheer into a cheerless house. Laurie didn't know that alcoholism was what made her mother tearful one moment and giddy the next. My inconsistency caused feelings of insecurity that she was too young to identify. She only knew that something was wrong, and she wanted to fix it. Laurie was playing the role of Family Hero, described by author Sharon Wegscheider in her study of the effects of alcoholism on children.[2] Wegscheider found that firstborn children of alcoholics often take on this role, discounting themselves by putting others first. My daughter was the classic example of the Family Hero: the helper, the consoler, and good student.

Some children play the role of the Lost Child—the one who withdraws, suppresses his feelings, and goes it alone. Too often the Lost Child buries his good feelings along with his hurts and grows into a joyless adulthood. Another child in the alcoholic family may take on the role of Scapegoat, the kid who is constantly in trouble, acting out his pain by defiance and hostility. He would rather get the negative attention his bad behavior elicits than no attention at all. The Scapegoat is often the most likely to become addicted to alcohol or drugs as an adult.

There are other roles that children learn to play on the stage of the alcoholic home, chosen as they discover ways that work for them in their search for some stability. The particular role a child chooses may be determined by chance, by his place in the family structure, or by inherent personality traits. Whatever his defense, it always proves an inadequate shield against the fear and confusion of an alcoholic home. The pain penetrates the mask and is carried into adulthood.

If the nonalcoholic parent can find help from a therapist who understands alcoholism or a support group like Al-Anon, he or she will have an opportunity to break the destructive interaction in the family and give the children a better chance of becoming emotionally stable adults. However, there is no denying that growing up in an alcoholic household will have a lasting and perhaps profound effect upon the lives of the children.

RESIDUAL PAIN

Adult children of alcoholics are beginning to bring their parent's alcoholism out of the closet and look at the continuing impact the disease has had on their lives. Now they are coming together in fellowships and organizations like ACA (Adult Children of Alcoholics, affiliated with Al-Anon), and NACA (National Association for Children of Alcoholics).

> The Children of Alcoholics (COAs)—loosely or-ganized but rapidly growing throughout the United States—reaffirm all of the previous grass-roots move-ments and bring us new insight into alcoholism's

effects on the more than 28 million Americans who have seen at least one parent in the throes of the affliction.[3]

Five years ago there were 21 people in an organization called the National Association for Children of Alcoholics; today [1988] there are more than 7,000. The 14 Al-Anon children-of-alcoholics groups meeting in the early '80s have increased to 1,100.[4]

Like members of Alcoholics Anonymous, they follow the Twelve-Step Program as they work through emotional pain left over from a troubled youth. In a home where a parent's alcoholism demanded center stage, their own needs had too often been unrecognized and unresolved. As these "adult children" find understanding and support in a group of people like themselves, they begin to erase the scars of their pasts.

What kinds of problems do these children have as adults?

Janet Geringer Woititz has identified thirteen traits that most children from alcoholic households experience to some degree. These symptoms, she says, can pose lifelong problems. According to her popular book, *Adult Children of Alcoholics*, they

- guess what normal behavior is.
- have difficulty following a project from beginning to end.
- lie when it would be just as easy to tell the truth.
- judge themselves without mercy.
- have difficulty having fun.
- take themselves very seriously.

- have difficulty with intimate relationships.
- overreact to changes over which they have no control.
- constantly seek approval and affirmation.
- feel that they are different from other people.
- are super-responsible or super-irresponsible.
- are extremely loyal, even in the face of evidence that the loyalty is undeserved.
- tend to lock themselves into a course of action without giving consideration to consequences.[5]

As these "adult children" meet together, they share their struggles and help one another deal with the leftover pain that affects their adult lives. As a group, they have discovered they have a lot in common. Most of them experience

- feelings of isolation,
- fear of people and authority figures,
- loss of their own identities as they strive to be people-pleasers,
- fear of personal criticism,
- an attraction to addictive personalities or fellow "victims,"
- a tendency to be concerned with others as a way of avoiding a closer look at themselves,
- feelings of guilt when they stand up for themselves instead of giving in to others,
- inability to differentiate between love and pity, a tendency to love people they can rescue,
- an inclination to "stuff" the feelings from their traumatic childhoods and a diminished ability to feel or express emotion,

- low self-esteem,
- the tendency to see issues as either black or white, and
- the tendency to react rather than act.

"Most of us are ultra-dependent personalities who are scared to death of being abandoned," said Lorna, a member of ACA. "We cling to people. Our emotional needs have gone unnoticed and unmet by our alcoholic parents, and we're still trying to fill that void by demanding too much from the people in our lives today. We all have hang-ups that show up in our current relationships."

Many adult children of alcoholics agree with her. They see themselves as emotional cripples who have been unable to form and maintain satisfying relationships with others. They have come to understand that alcoholism is a family disease that affects each member. They identify themselves as co-dependents who took on the characteristics of that disease, whether or not they ever picked up a drink.

Growing up is tough enough in the strongest of families. In a home where one or both parents are alcoholics, growing up emotionally may be an impossibility. But there is hope. With alcoholism "out of the closet," troubled adults are beginning to recognize and deal with feelings previously denied—feelings of hurt and anger and shame and bewilderment that arose during a childhood in an alcoholic family and found no place to be resolved.

A HEAD START

There are increasing opportunities for children of alcoholics to find support and understanding before becoming adults, thereby getting a head start on their own recoveries. Ala-Teen, a program for older children of alcoholics, has more than three thousand groups across the country and has been responsible for helping thousands of young people. Knowing that they are not alone and that there are others with whom they can share their confusion and fear helps them to focus on their own journeys through adolescence. Children Are People (CAP) is an organization geared to children of alcoholics ages 5 to 13. It was founded in St. Paul, Minnesota, in 1977 by Rokelle Lerner and Barbara Naditch and has counseled and supported more than 5,000 youngsters in that area. There are similar programs in San Francisco and Dallas.[6]

For the reader who is currently struggling with the effects of alcoholism on his family, this has been a sad chapter. It has been sad for the writer, as well, as my husband and I take an honest look at the years when our children were small and our separate marriages were failing because of rampant alcoholism. Repercussions of those years are affecting our children's lives today.

Two of our nine children have the disease of alcoholism: one is recovering; the other is still in denial. Five of our nine grew up to marry sons or daughters of alcoholics. One daughter-in-law is a recovering alcoholic. Our family did not escape the statistical probabilities.

Experience has shown me that people who grow up in dysfunctional homes often demonstrate superior moral fortitude and integrity. Some are a blessing to family and friends because of their unusual sensitivity to people around them and their willingness to help. Many have a great capacity for nurturing. Others have made important contributions to society.

As more and more public figures tell their stories of early years in the shadow of a parent's alcoholism, we can take hope from their victories. We don't have to look further than former President Ronald Reagan to be reassured that sons and daughters of alcoholics can overcome past hurts and be strengthened in the process.

As we watch our own children live out their adult lives, I thank God that their scars are less obvious than the strengths of character they developed in spite of our disease. Like other adult children of alcoholics they are survivors—resilient people who have the ability to bounce back from hardship and misfortune. We watch them "flex" with life's demands and rise above their circumstances and we are grateful and proud.

A few of our children have reached snags in their lives where they have had to confront past painful experiences and work on resolving the emotional conflicts that are interfering with their adult lives. Perhaps each one of them will come to a time of reckoning as they continue to mature. In the meantime, most of them have philosophically accepted the blight of alcoholism that affected their young lives and rejoice that their parents are sober today. The best news of all is that most of our children have come to know Jesus Christ as Lord of their lives, and He has made them new creatures with the power to overcome the enemy of their childhood.

For the children in our case studies—Brian, Eric, Stacy, and the rest—their hope, as ours, is in the grace of God. As a Christian, I claim for each of them God's promise: "I will repay you for the years the locusts have eaten" (Joel 2:25).

SUMMARY

- Alcoholic parents are unable to give their children the security and stability necessary for healthy character development.

- The nonalcoholic parent becomes as emotionally ill as the alcoholic and is apt to do as much damage to the children as the alcoholic himself.

- Children of alcoholics often lose their own identities as they take on roles that help them cope within the dysfunctional home.

- When and if the alcoholic parent becomes sober, the scars of the children remain.

- Adult children of alcoholics may have character traits carried over from childhood that trouble them as adults.

- Adult children of alcoholics are forming support groups to recognize and deal with feelings previously denied.

- With God's healing grace, children of alcoholics can overcome their painful pasts and go forward into satisfying and productive adulthood.

"Where Do We Turn For Help?"

Whether or not our stories in the previous chapters have convinced you that alcoholism is a true disease, you can probably see that a drinking problem won't vanish by itself. You will see that

- The alcoholic has gone beyond choice and is helplessly trapped by his addiction.
- Those close to the alcoholic suffer as much and often become as ill as the alcoholic.
- Family members and loved ones usually do the wrong things and help perpetuate the disease.

"So what is a family to do?"

There are three positive steps that you and others close to the alcoholic in your life can take to improve your situation:

1. Pray for wisdom.

2. Find ways to help yourself.
3. Intervene and confront.

BEGIN WITH PRAYER

First, you will need to undergird your efforts with prayer for wisdom and courage. To attempt to rescue someone from the clutches of drug addiction (and let's not forget that alcohol is a drug) is to engage in spiritual warfare. Maintaining your own sanity will be a challenge. For starters, listen to the words of The Serenity Prayer, used by anonymous self-help groups everywhere:

> *God grant me the serenity*
> *To accept the things I cannot change,*
> *Courage to change the things I can*
> *And the wisdom to know the difference.*
>   *Reinhold Niebuhr*

I know. You think serenity is beyond hope, and you can't and won't accept things as they are. Something had better change, you say, or you will lose your mind. You've tried and tried to change this *person* who is disrupting your life, but it hasn't worked. You're not sure you even care anymore. The love you once felt is dissolving in frustration and bitterness. And sometimes you wonder if God has forgotten you. We who have agonized over an alcoholic loved one understand.

However, you must have a shred of hope or you wouldn't be reading this book. With courage you *can* change some things that will make a difference in your life. Thousands of people like you have found a way to be happy and productive in spite of the alcoholics in their lives. They have survived their private wars, and so will you. By using the tools offered by these veterans, you can learn to accept some things and change others.

That brings us to the second step in the helping process. This involves helping yourself. Like other co-dependents, you have probably become so focused on the drinking problem that is affecting your life that you have become ill yourself. In order to be effective in this spiritual battle, you must achieve some emotional distance and objectivity.

Men and women whose lives are being torn apart by an alcoholic close to them find understanding and help in Al-Anon, the counterpart to Alcoholics Anonymous. Al-Anon is a program of recovery for the wives, husbands, relatives, and close friends of alcoholics. They believe that alcoholism is a family disease, and they meet to share their "experience, strength, and hope" with each other. Their purpose is to learn how to live comfortably in spite of the effects of the disease of alcoholism.

SHIFTING FOCUS

The Al-Anon fellowship has been invaluable to those who, before the program, had only been able to stand by and watch until their loved ones were ready for help. Here, in a compassionate group of men and women like themselves, the suffering family members learn there is very little they can *do* about the alcoholic. There are lots of *dos* for themselves and some suggested *don'ts* in regard to the alcoholic. Although he may have come to Al-Anon to find a way to change the alcoholic in his life, the newcomer soon learns that he is there for himself. His focus gradually shifts from the alcoholic's behavior to his own. Changing his own life is the only thing over which he has control.

As he takes charge of his own attitudes and reactions,

the destructive patterns of interaction within the family will begin to change. He will find that he has the power to bring a measure of stability to his home situation. In this healthier atmosphere, the alcoholic may come to realize her own condition and be willing to seek treatment. The ideal outcome of a family member's participation in the Al-Anon fellowship is serenity for himself and sobriety for his alcoholic. It doesn't always happen. However, at the very least, Al-Anon provides the support and understanding every victim of someone else's alcoholism so desperately needs. And each step short of total success is a lightening of the burden for the one who suffers because of another's addiction.

I have been amazed at the number of suffering souls who have resisted taking advantage of this valuable program. Janet is a case in point.

At her first Al-Anon meeting, Janet's voice was husky with unshed tears as she spoke. "I didn't want to come here," she said. "I still don't know what I'm doing here. I've tried everything anyone can possibly imagine to stop John from drinking so much. He'd cut down if he cared about us. He's jeopardizing his career, driving away our friends, and making nervous wrecks of me and the kids. I don't have the strength or the desire to fight it any more. Our lives have revolved around John and his craziness for too long, and I'm sick of it. *He's* the one who ought to be going for help, not me! I'm not the one with the problem."

Janet was in the right place to vent her frustration and anger. She was in the right place, too, to learn that alcoholism is a disease over which neither she nor John had control.

"That was like a revelation to me," she said later. "Of course, I had heard alcoholism referred to as a disease, but

I hadn't realized that term had anything to do with us. Alcoholism applied to those poor souls lined up at the mission for a Thanksgiving handout or to the drunk sleeping it off on a park bench, didn't it? How could a man like John—successful in his profession, respected by his peers, living in a good neighborhood—be in the same class as the transients I saw hanging around the bus station, panhandling for their next bottle of cheap wine? I'd come into the meeting full of anger at John, but I didn't want anyone to think he was *that* bad."

The men and women of Al-Anon understood Janet's reluctance to label John an alcoholic. Many of us (even those who accepted the label for ourselves) felt the same way in the beginning. Denial is a normal defense mechanism, a classic symptom of our distress. If we had admitted to alcoholism in ourselves or our loved one, it would have meant letting go of all control. And to surrender control was to lose all hope for change, we thought.

CONFUSING SIGNALS

"John couldn't be *alcoholic*," Janet told the Al-Anon group. "He may have a problem sometimes, but it's more likely when he's under a lot of pressure at work. And our son Jed has been giving us fits ever since he turned sixteen. John had quit drinking altogether for a couple of months until Jed started acting up. I'm sure he could do it again."

Most alcoholics will experience brief intervals of sobriety or periods of "controlled" drinking even as their disease progresses. Those who care find renewed hope at times like these. But the reprieve is almost always temporary and disappointment is just around the corner.

"When John found out that I'd gone to an Al-Anon meeting he was furious," said Janet. "He set out to show me that he had no problem cutting back. He switched from vodka to wine and only drank a couple of glasses of sherry before dinner. He made a big point of 'giving up the hard stuff to please the little woman.' It was a great act. After a couple of weeks, I found the empty vodka bottles in the basement. All I'd accomplished by going to Al-Anon, it seemed, was to drive him underground. Literally. But I was running out of defenses for John's behavior. And I'd heard enough in the few meetings I'd attended. I began to see that he had all the signs of addiction after all."

With her defenses down, Janet realized that she needed help for herself, no matter what John thought and whether or not he continued to drink. "Eventually it sunk in," Janet said. "I found out that the disease of alcoholism is contagious and insidious and that I had become ill from the effects of John's addiction. The frustration of trying to control his drinking, of covering up to friends and family (his parents and mine), of gradually taking over all the responsibilities of our household had made me as emotionally sick as he was. Al-Anon didn't give me advice, but they provided me with tools for rebuilding my own deteriorating life."

Janet learned that she no longer had to participate in John's battle with alcoholism. She learned that she hadn't caused his disease and that she was not responsible for his recovery from it.

"This is where 'changing the things I can' comes in," Janet said. "John wasn't on the list of things I could change. I had no choice but to stay miserable or change myself and my reactions to John's behavior. It wasn't easy, but my new friends showed me that it was an attainable goal."

From men and women like herself—spouses, sons

and daughters, parents, and friends of alcoholics—Janet learned the skill of *detachment* and slowly regained control over her own life. Members of Al-Anon learn

- not to suffer because of the actions or reactions of other people,
- not to allow themselves to be used or abused in the interest of another's recovery,
- not to do for others what they should do for themselves,
- not to manipulate situations so others will eat, go to bed, get up, pay bills, etc.,
- not to cover up for another's mistakes or misdeeds,
- not to create a crisis, and
- not to prevent a crisis if it is in the natural course of events.

Detachment is neither kind nor unkind. It does not imply evaluation of the person or situation from which we are detaching. It is simply a means for us to recover from the adverse effects of the disease of alcoholism upon our lives. Detachment helps families look at their situations realistically and objectively, thereby making intelligent decisions possible.[1]

"How can detachment help the alcoholic?"

Backing off, or "letting go and letting God" as the Al-Anon slogan goes, may help the frustrated family member, but does it really help the alcoholic? To some of us, detachment seemed more like deserting our responsibility to an alcoholic spouse. How does it fit with the biblical admonitions: "Husbands, love your wives, and do not be harsh with them" (Col. 3:19) or "Wives, submit to your husbands as to the Lord" (Eph. 5:22)?

Here is the testimony of a recovering alcoholic who was invited to speak to the local Al-Anon group:

"My name is Charlotte W. and I'm an alcoholic. A grateful alcoholic. Grateful to be sober and grateful to have the opportunity to stand before you tonight and help you, perhaps, to better understand the alcoholic in your life. I know what some of you are thinking: 'Who wants to?' Right? Well, I'm sure most of you are here because someone like me is driving you crazy. I'm not saying 'someone like I used to be,' because I think I'm still driving Walt crazy sometimes. He's back there in the corner, one of you, still recovering, as I am, from the effects of alcohol on his life.

"It's God's miracle that we're both here today—that we're anywhere at all together. Not very long ago there was more hate than love in our house. Hate is an ugly word, but alcoholism is an ugly disease. Walt hated me because I was ruining what started out to be a great marriage. He hated me because I was killing myself, and the part of him that still loved me didn't want me to die. He hated me"— Charlotte's voice broke a little—"because I was causing our wonderful children to suffer more than kids have any business suffering. They're recovering, too, by the grace of God and the Ala-teen meeting next door.

"So okay, I'll try to tell you what I was like and what happened, and you can judge for yourselves—or ask Walt—what I'm like now. The Bible tells us to seek first the kingdom of God and His righteousness and that's going to be my lifetime quest. That's my faith. 'God as I understand Him' is the God of the Bible—the Father-Creator who provided a Savior for lost souls like mine and a Comforter to come alongside me in my daily walk. I've returned to the faith of my childhood. As a little girl I loved Sunday school. In my child's imagination I connected God the Father with my own father and Jesus with my older brother Glen, whom I adored.

"When I was ten, Glen put on a uniform and went to Korea. He promised to write me lots of letters, but he only wrote one. By the time that arrived in the mail we'd already had the telegram telling us that he'd been killed in action. After that my dad drank a lot. One night he left the house drunk and drove over a cliff. My tender faith died along with my earthly heroes. Actually, I let it die because I was mad at God. That was my first bad choice.

"After that I made a lot of bad choices, like getting pregnant at sixteen and having an abortion. My friends drank, so it wasn't surprising that I did, too, but *no one* drank like I did. When I discovered that booze made life bearable, I pursued the next drink with all the determination of a starving animal after his next meal. I was, as they say, programmed for the disease of alcoholism. I was full of anger and fear and sorrow and guilt and a bunch of other things that all young people are plagued with at some time or another. Some of us manage to grow through the pain and some of us don't. I didn't like the maturing process and I didn't want to go any further into a future that couldn't be trusted. I felt there was probably some unknown horror waiting for me in the weeks and years to come. You can see what happened to my faith.

"I had some emotional problems and some personality traits that set me up for the disease of alcoholism, but the deciding factor for me, I'm convinced, was that my father was an alcoholic and I had inherited his genes. I didn't realize he was an alcoholic until I learned about alcoholism, but now I understand that he was. If he hadn't been killed at forty-three, he might have found the way out, as I have.

"Now, somewhere along the line I stayed sober enough for long enough to go to school and launch a career and meet Walt. He was the best thing that ever happened to me, and I had the temporary sense to know that. I went on the wagon for a few years after we were married and while we were having our babies. I thank God for that. Some of you have seen children with FAS (Fetal Alcohol Syndrome), victims of the effects of alcohol on the unborn fetus when a pregnant lady drinks. It is only by the grace of God that I had put my drinking on hold for the first few years of my marriage. But then life got tough and I went back to my magic cure-all for unhappiness.

"It wasn't anything major, like someone dying, but Walt changed jobs and we had to move and he worked longer hours and wasn't there to carry part of the load with our three preschoolers and I had a falling-out with a neighbor who'd been a good friend and we started socializing with Walt's new business associates and going to cocktail parties. I've always felt awkward and uncomfortable in unfamiliar surroundings—especially when I'm supposed to make conversation with strangers. Maybe that's true of all alcoholics. Maybe it's true of everyone. Maybe that's why cocktails are such a necessity at parties like that. You people are probably like Walt. He managed to enjoy himself just standing around talking to people. Sometimes he'd have half a highball and then set his glass down and forget it. He'd usually get tired and be ready to go home about the time I'd loosened up and was ready to make a night of it. I could usually find someone in the crowd who took drinking as seriously as I did. That made for strained relations on the home front.

"They say it takes several years of drinking before someone crosses the line into alcoholism. If so, I'm an exception. I picked up right where I'd left off in my single years and within a few months I had a full-fledged PROBLEM. And in my way of thinking it was my problem and no one else's. For the life of me I couldn't see why it should bother Walt if I had a few drinks in the afternoon while the kids were down for their naps, or later while they were at school. I didn't run around and drink in bars or anything like that. I was always home, wasn't I? He had clean underwear and socks in his drawers, didn't he? And wasn't supper always on the table when he *finally* came home at night? By the time I got through reciting the list of duties I performed and sacrifices I made for my family, I was feeling pretty sorry for myself and certainly justified in having another drink or two.

"I see some of you shaking your heads in wonder at my reasoning. I don't blame you. Looking at it with a sober eye, I wonder where my head was. But I know where my head was. An alcoholic will go to any lengths to justify and rationalize his drinking. We deceive ourselves because we must drink. Somewhere along the line we've lost the power of choice. We can't admit that to ourselves and we wouldn't dream of admitting it to you because then you might do something about it, like take our booze away. We are *so* afraid of what you might do about our drinking problem!

"I'll bet I can guess some of the things you've done about your alcoholic's drinking problem:

"You tore the house apart until you found where she was hiding her bottles—at the bottom of the laundry basket in the basement, in an old boot at the back of her closet, behind the encyclopedias in the den. Did you ever wonder why alcoholics buy those little bottles of booze? Because they're easier to hide, that's why.

"You confronted her with the evidence and then tortured her by pouring it down the drain. Then, to shut her up, you went out and bought her another bottle. 'We'll keep this one in the kitchen,' you said, 'and we'll have a drink together before supper.' You thought that was working until you found another empty under the mattress in the guest room.

"You made excuses to your friends when he made a public fool of himself at their anniversary party. You told them the dentist had given him some medication for an infected tooth, and you guessed it didn't mix with the wine at dinner. 'So sorry about the broken window,' you had said. You'd call the glass company in the morning and send someone out to fix it. Then you ranted and raved at him all the way home and made him sleep on the couch in the den.

"You called his office in the morning and told his boss that he seemed to have a touch of the flu again and he wouldn't want to expose the rest of the gang to it. Then you gave him the silent treatment for the rest of the day.

"You followed him around at the next party and counted his drinks and wondered why he got so out of control after only two or three and then were furious when you found out he got a head start while you were in the shower.

"You nagged her about what she was doing to her health and how she was neglecting the kids and the house and her friends and you, and then you told her you didn't give a damn what she did and slammed out of the house.

"And then . . .

"You took the opposite approach, treating her with kid gloves and confusing her with kindness, acting as if everything was fine and wonderful. You decided you were somehow at fault. If you were a good enough wife or husband or daughter or father, your alcoholic wouldn't drink so much. And so you tried to be better, kinder, more helpful, more understanding.

"And what happened? Nothing. It didn't matter what you did or didn't do, whether you were angry or tolerant. If you tried to control our drinking, we fought you all the way. If you pretended that nothing was wrong, we sensed the phoniness and knew that it was just another device to control us. As long as you involved yourselves with or intruded upon our drinking careers, we fought.

"Now you people out there somehow got smart or maybe got desperate enough to find other victims like yourselves and find out what they are doing about their lives. Walt heard about Al-Anon from a man at the shop. This guy (Ed was his name) had a wife who called him six times a day in hysterics about one thing or another, and Walt thought the poor guy would give up and quit the job or leave town or go crazy or something. Then he noticed that Ed's attitude was changing. He didn't look quite so hang-dog when he came to work in the morning. He was calmer and more cheerful, and when his wife called he kept his cool—at least on the surface. One day Walt came to work feeling very discouraged about my drinking, and he told Ed a little of what was going on. Before that he hadn't let on to *anyone* that there was trouble in paradise. Ed shared with him his own story, about how frustrated he was with his wife's alcohol problem and how Al-Anon had helped him. It hasn't, so far, made a difference to Ed's

wife—she's still 'out there,' as we say in AA—but Walt's
going to Al-Anon was the beginning of the end for me.
The end of the bad time and the beginning of a new way of
life.

"This is what happened. Walt stopped counting my
drinks, stopped making excuses for me, stopped lecturing
me. One night coming home from a PTA meeting (Can
you believe I was still doing things like that?) I missed the
driveway by a couple of feet and collided with our mailbox.
Walt didn't see the crumpled fender until the next
morning, and then he didn't say anything—just left the
number of Earl's Body Shop by the phone with instruc-
tions for me to ask for Red and *not* to call the insurance
company. He left it up to me to explain what happened if
anyone should ask. When I forgot some appointment we'd
made together, he'd either go without me or expect me to
call and make my own apologies.

"Do you know how this made me feel? Abandoned,
that's how. Deserted. Desperate. Like our daughter Gina
the first time she went in the pool without her water wings.
It was sink or swim time for me. Walt was still there and I
knew it, but he wasn't fighting me any more.

"You know, as long as we have life we have some
element of choice. We alcoholics lose our power of choice
once we take that first drink, but there are those times
between binges, even for a daily drinker like I was, when
we can choose to get off the merry-go-round and ask for
help. I was sober—relatively sober anyway—when I woke
up in the morning. I'd lie there in bed and make promises
to myself, knowing I wasn't going to keep them but making
vows to change, to be a better wife and mother, to stop
drinking so much. I knew that I'd break my promises

because I knew that I didn't have the power to keep them. And I hadn't yet chosen to reach out for help.

"I could always blame Walt. As long as he was involving himself in my drinking activities, he couldn't do anything right. And of course it was easy for me to blame my unhappiness on him and his criticizing or his patronizing or whatever he was trying at that stage of my drinking. When he backed off and stopped doing anything at all, it put the problem right back in my lap where it belonged. He was just so cool, you wouldn't believe it. I know now that he wasn't all that serene underneath, but he did *nothing* to support my martyrdom.

"I came to a point where I couldn't blame anyone or anything for what was happening to me. I had to admit I was sick and getting sicker every day. Apparently no one was going to rescue me from my bondage to alcohol. Somehow I'd have to do it myself. That's what I finally said to myself on one of those relatively sober mornings, *I'll have to do it myself.* Then I said, *But I can't do it! God, You know I've tried and I can't do it!* God was listening.

"Well, that's the beginning of recovery for each of us alcoholics. Admitting our slavery. Our helplessness. We had to admit, as the First Step says, that we were 'powerless over alcohol, that our lives had become unmanageable.' And if I was powerless over alcohol, the only choice I had was to drown in it or get it out of my life. Oh boy, that's the hardest thing I ever did. Fortunately, I knew something about AA. A girl I used to work with had a sister who'd joined. I'd known about her and about the fact that she'd had to quit drinking altogether. I didn't want to go that route, but I didn't want to keep on the way I was going either, so I thought I'd look into it.

"I wish I could say that our problems were solved

from that day forward. I was a hard case, and I kept trying to find another way. Giving up my booze entirely was too painful, and I wasn't good at pain. So I'd have sober periods where I'd go around like a martyr, needing lots of pats on the back and being just as hard to live with as when I was drinking. During these intervals, it was just a matter of time before I started drinking again, and I had everyone walking on eggs in anticipation of my next slip. Poor Walt. At least when I was drinking every day he had some idea of what to expect. I'd gone from the merry-go-round of daily drinking to the see-saw of periodic binges. It was a devil's playground. But Walt was learning about detaching, as you people so aptly put it. When he got out from under the oppression of my addictive disease, he freed me to take responsibility for myself. If Walt hadn't had your support here in Al-Anon, he never would have made it. And if he hadn't been able to keep his cool, I might not have made it either.

"I want to thank you for your part in my sobriety. In helping Walt, you helped me more than you can know. As I said in the beginning, I'm a grateful alcoholic. Grateful to my Lord who led me to AA and Walt to Al-Anon. Grateful to each of you who are here for us. Thank you all."

That's how Walt's participation in Al-Anon helped hasten Charlotte's recovery from addiction. Her humble testimony validates the effectiveness of this program.

"But is Al-Anon a Christian program?"

Like Alcoholics Anonymous, Al-Anon is a spiritual program for people who are suffering from the effects of alcohol on their lives. Although members are urged to believe in and trust a Power greater than themselves, they are free to form their own individual concepts of this

Higher Power. Some newcomers to the program have been embittered and turned off by judgmental "religious" leaders and friends to whom they had once turned for help; some have never had a strong faith of any kind; some are Christians and have no doubts about the identity of their Higher Power. Wherever they are spiritually, Al-Anon (like AA) is there to bring aid and comfort to their wounds. Is there any doubt that God blesses such a program?

The fact that AA and Al-Anon profess a somewhat vague spirituality is not a problem for those who know Whom they have believed; for others the program often serves as a spiritual kindergarten, as it did for Janet.

"The words in Step Three of the Twelve Steps, 'God *as we understood Him*,' kept echoing in my head," said Janet. "I did have some picture of God as a supreme being, and my striving to bring Him closer in my desperate need of His help led me eventually to a personal relationship with Jesus Christ. If John had never gotten sober, if nothing else in my life had ever changed, knowing God— really knowing Him—was worth all the agony of the years before."

The Twelve Steps, originated by founding fathers of Alcoholics Anonymous and utilized by Al-Anon, Overeaters Anonymous, Gamblers Anonymous, Narc-Anon, and many other anonymous programs throughout the world are solid biblical principles restated. They ask us to begin by taking an honest look at ourselves and our relationships with others; they guide us through a process of dying to self and finding hope and strength in reliance on God.

Here are the steps that have helped lead thousands out of despair and into a new way of life:

THE TWELVE STEPS

1. We admitted we were powerless over alcohol—that our lives had become unmanageable.

2. Came to believe that a Power greater than ourselves could restore us to sanity.

3. Made a decision to turn our will and our lives over to the care of God *as we understood Him.*

4. Made a searching and fearless moral inventory of ourselves.

5. Admitted to God, to ourselves, and to another human being the exact nature of our wrongs.

6. Were entirely ready to have God remove all these defects of character.

7. Humbly asked Him to remove our shortcomings.

8. Made a list of all persons we had harmed, and became willing to make amends to them all.

9. Made direct amends to people wherever possible, except when to do so would injure them or others.

10. Continued to take personal inventory and when we were wrong promptly admitted it.

11. Sought through prayer and meditation to improve our conscious contact with God *as we understood Him,* praying only for knowledge of His will for us and the power to carry that out.

12. Having had a spiritual awakening as the result of these Steps, we tried to carry this message to others, and to practice these principles in all our affairs.[2]

A wise Christian reminded me once that "truth is truth wherever you find it." God's truth within the spiritual program of Al-Anon is confirmed in its healing power. If you are a Christian in need of help because of the problem drinker in your life, don't be afraid to seek help in Al-Anon. You may not hear talk of the Lord Jesus there, but you will hear words of hard-won wisdom from people who have stood where you stand today. You may flinch sometimes at the rough language, but you will be uplifted and inspired by the courageous victories of those who are learning to overcome the despair that brought them to the group. Remember that each of these people is beloved of God. Each has opened himself to the possibility that trust in God can help heal him. Can we not trust the Lord to bring him the rest of the way?

"Where do confrontation and intervention come in?"

Sometimes direct confrontation of the alcoholic can follow close on the heels of the first two steps, suggested at the beginning of this chapter. If your alcoholic is dying before your eyes, it's pretty hard to be patient and concentrate on your own recovery. *Intervention* can be an effective and successful weapon in the battle against addiction. Former First Lady Betty Ford's highly publicized recovery from alcohol and prescription drug dependence began with the technique of intervention, a process pioneered by the Johnson Institute in Minnesota.

The purpose of intervention is, of course, to help the alcoholic face his progressive addiction and the devastating effect it is having on his life and the lives of people he cares about. Surrounded by people who love him enough to confront him with simple facts without berating him or preaching to him in moralistic tones, he may be able to admit his need for help.

> Confronting the addict all at once with a number of family members, close friends, and authorities (job supervisor, family doctor, pastor), who describe his or her behavior in specific detail, but in a loving and nonjudgmental atmosphere, helps break down the addict's walls of denial.[3]

Professionals with whom I've spoken tell me that this is an extremely sensitive technique and must be handled with great delicacy if it is to be successful. Poorly planned interventions have been known to have disastrous consequences.

Before attempting such a confrontation, there are important guidelines that must be followed.

1. **Seek direction** and leadership from a qualified counselor who understands alcoholism and is familiar with the intervention process. It is important to have a leader who can remain objective during the confrontation when tears may flow and tempers flare.
2. **Choose members** of the intervention team who have a close relationship to the alcoholic and who are willing to participate. These will be family members, close friends, business associates—anyone who is affected by and concerned about the drinking problem and is willing to help.
3. **Prepare the evidence.** Each member of the team will be expected to present two or three examples of the alcoholic's inappropriate and unacceptable behavior while under the influence of alcohol. In presenting

these examples, the participants should use "I" statements—"I was embarrassed when you made a pass at my fiancé at our engagement party," rather than "You made an idiot of yourself at our engagement party." The purpose of this presentation is not to humiliate the alcoholic but to help him see the seriousness of the situation. A rehearsal of the actual dialogue is strongly recommended.

4. **Have a treatment plan** ready. If the alcoholic even reluctantly accepts his need for help, immediate action is called for. Three alternative methods of treatment recommended by professionals are: a thirty-day inpatient program at an alcoholism rehabilitation center, an outpatient program at an alcoholism treatment facility, or attendance at ninety AA meetings in ninety days.

If the alcoholic can be made to see that his health, his job, and his relationships are truly in jeopardy; if he can be led to understand the effect that his behavior has had upon those he cares about; and if he can come to this realization in an atmosphere of understanding and love, he has a good chance for recovery.

Sometimes the initial intervention fails, or the alcoholic may accept treatment and then relapse. At this stage families need to bond together in prayer warfare. The authors of *Taking Control* advise families to form a "funnel" of loving confrontation.

At the top of the funnel is the status quo—the alcoholic or addict running the show, drinking, and losing his temper, and then being sober, and the family bouncing around and recoiling to whatever he or she does. The family is not in control; the addict is. Then there is the sickening crash as he or she eventually hits bottom.

Satan has had his heyday with the addict, so putting a ring of prayer around the addict and agreeing together to begin at the top of the funnel, one which will be slowly tightened with tough love, is the best approach. . . . Sometimes you may put conditions on relationships, sometimes withdrawing certain kinds of emotional support, sometimes actually distancing yourself from that person so that slowly it becomes less and less advantageous or even possible for him to abuse his addictive substance without negative consequences.[4]

The object of the "funnel," of course, is to narrow the alcoholic's options. Ultimately he may seek help for his addiction rather than risk losing the attention, care, and support he's previously received from family and friends.

THE BATTLE CONTINUES

Recovery from alcoholism is rarely a straight path. The initial joy you experienced at your alcoholic's surrender to sobriety may be quickly overshadowed by the difficulty of living with him during his transition to sobriety. He is learning to walk without his crutch. He will stumble often and fall occasionally. He may be moody, irritable, and self-centered, seemingly incapable of acting like a mature adult. You can expect frustrations and setbacks. You may find yourself thinking that you liked him better when he was drinking.

Now more than ever, you need support from those who have been where you are. You are still involved in spiritual warfare. You are still recovering from your own wounds. Recovery from alcoholism is not easy, for you or for the addicted one. Hang in there. Pray without ceasing. Reach out to those who are there to help you. A sober alcoholic is a miracle of God. His healing power is there for your loved one as it was for me and over a million others who lead happy, sober, productive lives.

The good news for each one of us, whatever our life struggles may be, is that God is able to save our lives from destruction. When choices made from ignorance or in rebellion to divine principles lead us into captivity, when we waste our gifts and talents in pursuit of harmful or meaningless goals, the final word has yet to be spoken about our lives. God can restore "the years the locusts have eaten" (Joel 2:25). He can turn our most grievous defeats into victory and our crippling weaknesses into an opportunity to experience his strength and mercy. Step by step, day by day, through repentance and in quiet service to the Lord, our broken lives can be transformed into glorious reflections of our Creator.[5]

SUMMARY

- Those close to the alcoholic suffer as much and often become as ill as the alcoholic.

- There are positive steps you can take to improve your situation.

- Undergird your efforts with prayer for wisdom and courage.

- Shifting your focus will help. Al-Anon can show you how.

- Intervention can be an effective tool against alcoholism.

- Recovery from alcoholism is rarely a straight path.

- God can work a miracle in your life.

"How Can We Help?"

Christ is the answer. We know that. He's God's solution to the evil in the world and the sin in our individual lives. Even so, when someone said those words to me—"Christ is the answer"—I didn't understand. I was grasping for a sobriety I didn't really want but desperately needed, and I didn't see how this advice could apply to my life.

As I've said, I had a private concept of God. He inhabited some other world full of good people who had managed to stay on the straight and narrow all their lives. That world didn't include me. Not knowing the kind of a God who would send his Son to die for the sin that He knew would rule my life, I thought I had failed to qualify for membership in His kingdom long ago. Christ might be the answer for hurting souls in that other world (innocent types who were hurting through no fault of their own), but I needed human beings. I needed directions for getting myself out of the mess I was in. I needed a plan of action.

"God, help me," I'd cried out to the God I didn't know, and He'd given me people to understand and comfort me. They told me they'd been where I was, and they lovingly led me out of the trap of addiction. They set my feet on a new path and told me that following some time-tested steps would help me grow spiritually. They talked about a Higher Power—God, as I understood Him—who was there for me to lean on while I stumbled along those steps. I looked at those kind souls, those repentant drunks who didn't fit my picture of "good" people, and found a new heart-image of God. I had taken the first step toward the spiritual growth they talked about in their Twelfth Step.

Eventually, of course, I came to know who God was and that He had been there always, waiting to shower His grace upon me. I understood at last that God had created the people I needed and put them within my reach. I understood that God was not just a Sunday person, but He'd been there on those Monday mornings when I couldn't remember the details of the night before. It was fourteen years between the day I'd cried out to God and the day I accepted Jesus Christ as Lord of my life, but my heart tells me that my spiritual conversion began with that first "foxhole" prayer. And at last I understood the meaning of the words: "Whosoever will may come."

"Couldn't an understanding minister have helped?"

Many times a compassionate and understanding minister has been able to help someone who is struggling with addiction to alcohol or other drugs. However, in almost every case where sobriety is achieved and maintained, the pastor has followed his own prayer and counsel with a referral to Alcoholics Anonymous or an alcoholic treatment facility. Unfortunately, too many church leaders mistrust any resource that isn't outspokenly Christian and attempt to take the entire burden of the alcoholic's recovery upon their own shoulders.

Some Christians look askance at organizations that speak of God in vague and general terms. One dear minister who was instrumental in leading me to Christ insisted that Alcoholics Anonymous was a cult and that I wouldn't have had a problem with alcohol if I'd been a Christian. Fortunately, I was not tempted to endanger my hard-won sobriety by testing his hypothesis. I fear for the alcoholic who embraces such a theory and uses it as an excuse to resume or continue drinking.

My pastor friend was mistaken in his judgment of AA. He'd heard rumors of new AA members being told to "use the group or a chair or this coffee pot here as your Higher Power. It doesn't matter, just so long as you have one." I've yet to hear of anyone in AA worshiping chairs or coffee pots. If such statements are made occasionally, they are probably intended to emphasize the complete lack of religious dogma within the program.

There is valid reason for the omission of theology in AA. The Christian founders of the program carefully and prayerfully drafted the Twelve Steps to include anyone who suffered from addiction to alcohol. The program's "God as you understand Him" approach is far more effective in the beginning stages of recovery than a declaration that "Christ is the answer." Too many alcoholics come to AA feeling misunderstood and rejected by their churches. Clinton White, author of *Wise Up! How?*, wrote:

Many well-meaning people don't understand that when they slap a derelict on the back and say, "God can help you," they might be opening some old wounds and be bringing back memories of some bitter disappointments.[1]

He goes on to tell about his quest for help from the clergy. One minister advised him to find a job chopping wood, another asked him to join his church, another told him he could become a normal drinker with proper counsel.

I would encourage all church leaders—ministers, elders, deacons—to familiarize themselves with the nature of alcoholism and with the program of Alcoholics Anonymous. The unprecedented success this fellowship has had in helping alcoholics recover from their addiction can serve as an inspiration to the local church. Open meetings can be found in almost every community. Interested visitors are always welcome. In addition to the 33,840 AA groups in the United States (62,860 known groups in 112 countries), there are more than a thousand treatment and rehabilitation centers whose facilities could be investigated and recommended by pastor-counselors. The church needs to recognize and consider utilizing the proven methods of secular groups in the treatment of alcoholism.

THE SPIRITUAL FLASH

You may know of someone who has found God and lost his craving for alcohol at the same time. It does happen, but it's the exception rather than the rule. More common are the stories about the town drunk who answers the altar call to be saved at every revival service and goes out to drink again. To old timers this was proof positive that the alcoholic was beyond help. Certainly God has the power to cure any disease at any stage of development, but only very rarely does He take away the craving for alcohol in a spiritual flash. God knows that most of us need to go through a painful process of recovery in order to grow in His image.

The church's attempts to help alcoholics failed miserably as long as the clergy's approach was to preach and pray the alcoholic out of his bondage to sin. Until God led a couple of desperate drunks to reach out to *each other* for help and to seek others who were fighting a losing battle for sobriety, alcoholics were usually given up as lost souls and hidden in shame. Given this well-publicized historical fact, isn't it a wonder that the clergy is still trying to cure the suffering alcoholic by waving the Bible at him and admonishing him to "go and sin no more"? Anderson Spickard, Christian Medical Director of the Vanderbilt Institute for Treatment of Alcoholism, writes:

> The implication is that addiction is strictly a spiritual problem, and that alcoholics and drug addicts who give themselves to God and faithfully attend church services and Bible studies will be cured of their problem.
>
> I identify deeply with this point of view because it was once my own, and I know it often springs from a deep concern and compassion for addicted people. At the same time, I have learned from painful experience that the search for a so-called Christian solution to the problem of addiction usually does more harm than good, and in a sad number of cases, it prevents alcoholics from getting the help they need.[2]

Our churches are full of people suffering from our disease. The most conservative estimates say that 6 percent of a congregation are likely to be alcoholics. We are out there in your midst and we are hurting. Some of us work hard to maintain a fragile sobriety. Others of us have achieved more stability, yet we will go to any lengths to hide our alcoholism from our church family. In greatest need are those who are still enslaved by their addictions and the families who suffer with them. We yearn for your understanding and fear your condemnation.

"How can we help you reach out to us?"

You need to know that we are sensitive to your attitudes toward us and our disease. We will find healing for our wounded spirits in your encouragement or be further wounded by your judgments. If, like many Christians, you feel that addiction is strictly a spiritual problem—sin, rather than sickness—your conviction will come across to us in subtle ways. We may still be struggling with the guilt that kept us on the merry-go-round of denial for so many years. In recovery we are told that alcoholism is a disease and not a moral issue, and we want to believe it. We hear you say things like: "We are all equal at the foot of the cross," but somehow we don't think your sin can be as bad as our own.

Recently I found a letter I'd written as a young Christian to the congregation of the church we were attending. I had hoped to find the courage to stand before my fellow believers and read it.

Dear Church Family,
    Tomorrow is New Year's Eve, another "watch night" in your tradition, and my husband and I look

forward to sharing it with you for the fourth year. I love to listen to your testimonies as you publicly praise God for His guidance in your lives. I love to listen to you, but my knees turn to Jello and my tongue to stone when I think about standing in front of you with my own testimony.

I can imagine the shock on your faces if I were to say, "I'm an alcoholic and I thank God that I no longer celebrate this holiday by getting drunk." Most of you grew up in homes where strong drink was forbidden, so it's understandable if you don't understand alcoholism. A few of you have children—young adults—who are problem drinkers, but I sense that the congregation considers them "fallen into sin" rather than suffering from a disease.

I am a sinner saved by grace. Those are familiar words, echoed by Christians everywhere. It is easy to stand before a Christian assembly and repeat that phrase. In so doing we identify with our brothers and sisters in Christ. We become more integrated with the body. Why, then, is it so difficult to be more specific about the sin in our lives? How often do we hear someone say, "I am a liar, a thief, an adulterer—a drunkard"? After five years in this church family, I tremble at the thought of revealing who I really am.

I am an alcoholic, rescued not by the church but by a program, a way of life, that I found in the secular world. That is the same as saying I am a sinner saved by grace because the grace of God engineered my rescue. I am sober today by the grace of God. My rescue from the illness of alcoholism and my spiritual regeneration took place outside the church. Eventually, having had a spiritual awakening, I sought a closer walk with God and was led to accept Jesus as my Lord and Savior. Only then did I become part of this church family. As a young Christian, I need you as a child needs his biological family. I need your understanding, your support, and your love. Christ calls us to bear one another's burdens. I ask you to share yours with me and to help me bear mine.

That was my letter, written eleven years ago. Cowardice prevailed and the "watch night" gathering didn't hear my testimony. I found it recently in a desk drawer, saved in case I might have the courage to read it the following year. But we left that church and those dear people before the year was up, not because of anything they did, but because of what I couldn't do—share myself with them.

A PASTOR'S PERSPECTIVE

Alexander DeJong, a former pastor and theologian, writes of his own apprehension in revealing his alcoholism to his congregation:

> I had been wrestling with the dilemma that is at the very core of alcoholism. Is it sin or is it sickness? For the longest time I believed it was sin; I was responsible for my own suffering. To many Christians, especially those that drink socially, this is a common way of thinking. They deal with alcohol entirely in terms of personal self-control, willpower, and moral discipline. To them an alcoholic should know better than to drink at the wrong time or excessively. Certainly, then, when people drink too much or become alcoholic, they are committing a sin; they are failing to control their appetite for alcohol.[3]

DeJong goes on to say:

The last thing most alcoholics need is a stronger sense of guilt. This is especially true for Christian alcoholics: most of them pray for forgiveness more frequently, urgently, and sincerely than most observers will ever know. The greatest needs of the alcoholic are likely to be hope, acceptance, understanding, and assurance of forgiveness. Veiled and sometimes insensitive judgment on the part of those who reject the disease concept of alcoholism can and often does lead to further tragic injury for wounded Christians already caught in the trap of this sickness. If one rejects the illness approach, it is nonetheless urgent to recall that the causes of addiction are so varied, so ill-defined that true Christian concern recommends quiet reservation and strong, accepting patience.[4]

"Should Christians drink at all?"

Whether or not to drink alcoholic beverages is a personal choice for every believer. Salvation does not hinge upon our habits. Seventy percent of Americans drink to some degree. Among Protestants, at least two-thirds now claim to drink at least socially. Our churches have softened the old "fire and brimstome" approach in their preaching in order to emphasize grace. Legalistic don'ts are overshadowed by the joy and freedom of salvation.

Christians in most denominations have become more integrated into their secular communities and have accepted many of the social customs of their neighbors. The Bible says we are to be "in the world." We are called to a life of temperance, not abstinence. The admonition against drunkenness is clear, but nowhere in the Bible does it say that Christians are to refrain from drinking alcoholic beverages. Jesus turned water into wine for his friends. Here in Southern California we are long on wine and short on water. If Jesus were here today, I wonder if he wouldn't zap away a few vineyards and create lakes and streams in their place.

A WARNING

If you choose to drink, you should know the risk. Ten percent of all drinkers (about 7 percent of the population) will eventually become problem drinkers or alcoholics. Christians are not immune. They are vulnerable to the same psychological and physiological factors that contribute to addiction in the nonbeliever. *Willpower will not prevent alcoholism.*

If there is alcoholism in your family, you are more at risk than the average social drinker. Remember that no one intentionally becomes addicted to alcohol. The more we alcoholics enjoyed the apparent benefits of a social drink, the more we fought for control. But we had passed the point of no return before we knew what was happening to us. It could happen to you.

Alcohol is a mood-altering drug. It can lift the tension that remains after a difficult day and offer a reprieve from the nagging worries that sometimes override faith and keep us from relaxing. For the introverted, self-conscious person who loses some of his stiffness after a drink or two, the positive effects of social drinking seem to outweigh the negative. Now that I am sober, I have to admit that I enjoy talking to someone at a party who is warmer toward me because of the drink in his hand. If he can handle it, more power to him. I had to give up the benefits he's obtaining from his social drink and let God teach me how to overcome my own self-consciousness and relate to other people.

Alcohol acts directly on the cerebrum to depress our inhibitions. There are times when these inhibitions work overtime and give us pain, and to have them depressed a bit seems like a good thing. But God created inhibitions for our protection. Without them we would lose control of our behavior and be more vulnerable than ever to the temptations that surround us. To forfeit our inhibitions is to take off the "full armor of God" that Paul writes about in the book of Ephesians. He warns us that

> Our struggle is not against flesh and blood, but against . . . the powers of this dark world and against the spiritual forces of evil in the heavenly realms.
>
> *(Eph. 6:12)*

"Can a morally strong person lose control and become alcoholic?"

A woman or man with strong morals and fine basic values can cross the line from social drinking to alcoholism and find herself behaving in ways that would have appalled her a short time before. He may lie, cheat, and steal in his business; she may neglect all responsibility to her family; he may fall into bed with a casual acquaintance. As her alcoholism progresses, she repeatedly violates her own code of ethics and is tormented by guilt. He tries to drown his painful memories in more alcohol and compounds the moral damage. It is a downward spiral. Knowing that this devastation can happen to the unsuspecting Christian may explain the old-time taboos against beverage alcohol.

While older Southern Baptists covenanted to "abstain

from the sale and use of intoxicating drinks," many churches of that denomination have now done away with that part of their covenant. Among younger members the legalistic restraints are coming down. My grandmother, a Methodist, would not have liquor in her house and would not tolerate drinking in her presence. Today's Methodists seem to be less rigid in their approach to social drinking. In my personal research, the only denomination I find taking a universal stand against the use of alcoholic beverages is the Salvation Army. All others seem to vary from congregation to congregation.

> Evangelicals, who used to be known primarily as a group of teetotalers, no longer hold that distinction. Many evangelicals, particularly upwardly mobile ones, now drink to stay socially relevant in their work and community situations. Acceptance of evangelicals into mainstream America has had the effect of evangelicals accepting many of mainstream America's social mores.[5]

I have no argument with a Christian brother or sister who chooses to drink socially. Most of you will never lose control of that freedom and have to go through the nightmare of addiction that I experienced. Most of you will not have the physiological reaction to alcohol that I had. But if statistics are reasonably accurate, some of you *will* fall into the trap of addiction. You must weigh that fact against the advantages if you choose to drink.

There is one other reason that you may decide not to drink. As Christians we stand before the world as witnesses to the power of God in our lives. No one wants to appear "holier than thou" or stand around at a cocktail party with raised eyebrows and pursed lips, but wouldn't it be great if we could shine with a special kind of joy?

William Lenters, addictions counselor and ordained minister, makes an astute observation:

> Both religion and alcohol offer an answer to weariness, boredom and drudgery, rejection and loneliness, fear, meaninglessness, and a sense of anomie. Bellying up to the bar for another glass of fire-brewed magic and shuffling up to the altar for the mystical host are not altogether unrelated motions. Camaraderie happens in the fellowship hall after the morning service and in the cocktail lounge during "happy hour." It was no accident that the newly anointed apostles on Pentecost morning were mistaken for common drunks on the street.[6]

If we could demonstrate a warmth and enthusiasm and delight in living that overflows from a vibrant faith, perhaps some who are seeking to fill their spiritual cups at the neighborhood bar might be drawn instead to our Source.

"Do some churches actually encourage drinking?"

As churches have become less stringent in their attitudes toward social drinking, believers have become liberated from legalistic restraints. Not only is it okay to drink, it's acceptable to serve alcohol at church-wide gatherings and even to offer drinks at prayer meetings. This brings the formerly restricted believer into a new area of vulnerability.

Jamie Buckingham wrote a powerful testimony of his own legalistic, teetotaling upbringing and his release from that legalism. He writes about "an experience with the Holy Spirit" at which time, he said, "Everything about me changed. He literally set me free." What followed was a relaxing of past standards that no longer seemed to fit with his new freedom, in particular a lifting of the ban against drinking alcoholic beverages.

> My new walk in the Spirit opened the door to a number of new associations as I realized—for the first time in my life—that Baptists did not have a corner on truth. I suddenly had a new respect for Pentecostals, Catholics, Nazarenes, Episcopalians—all had something worthwhile to offer me.
>
> It was a shock, being around these new friends. Jackie and I attended a prayer meeting in Tampa where cocktails were served. We had dinner with a small group of charismatics in our little town of Melbourne. All had wine with their meal. The Episcopal priest who ministered to me when I received the baptism in the Holy Spirit chided me, when I visited him later, saying I was "stiff" and "Baptistic." I needed to loosen up, have a few drinks, and enjoy God's elixer.[7]

That was the beginning of a time when Buckingham reexamined his attitude toward the use of alcohol for himself and for others. He had the freedom to join in with his new associates and, finally, as he realized that his behavior might prove a stumbling block for others, the freedom to choose *not* to drink. But he could have been one of the one in ten who are predisposed to alcoholism, and he could have lost the ability to return to the practice of abstinence.

Catholic, Lutheran, and Episcopal churches are

known in many communities as drinking churches, and the percentage of alcoholics in their congregations is apt to be higher than in the more conservative churches. "One startling statistic puts the percentage of Catholic priests who are alcoholic at 10 percent—about the same as in the general population. A Vatican ruling in 1983 required alcoholic priests to drink wine during Mass. For the previous decade a special permission had been given for such priests to use grape juice or simply not drink from the communion cup, but the special permissions were discontinued. An alcoholic priest I know was distressed by the new ruling. In his opinion it is placing many of his colleagues at unnecessary risk. Literally hundreds of priests are treated each year for alcoholism and many relapses are triggered by careless use of wine in the Mass.[8]

At some synod conventions within the Lutheran Church, wine and cheese parties are held regularly after the first evening's worship service. Drinks are served at congregational functions.

> "The Hospitality Hour," "The Welcoming Reception," and "The Friendship Time" are all code terms for cocktails before dinner. The need to describe these ecclesiastical happy hours with such thinly veiled euphemisms reveals the church's uncertainty about their propriety.[9]

THE ALCOHOLICS AMONG US

As the tide of alcoholism and other drug addiction rises, many churches are taking a closer look at their own attitudes toward social drinking. Church leaders—including those who decline to take a stand against the use of alcohol—don't willingly endorse a lifestyle that may contribute to the problems within their congregations. Unfortunately, they are often blind to the alcohol addiction that already exists among their members.

Vanessa was an active member of her church for all the years that her husband Wayne was drinking himself to death. Almost everyone in town knew that he had a drinking problem. Vanessa was close to her pastor and worked many hours as a volunteer in his office. She buried her pain beneath an effervescent personality and a ready smile.

"Didn't you ever tell him what was happening in your life?" I asked.

"Oh, no," said Vanessa, seemingly surprised at my question. "Pastor Rolf was such a busy man and carried too many burdens for the people in our congregation. To tell you the truth, I tried to spare him. Besides, he liked Wayne. Wayne didn't come to church very often because he was usually hung over on Sunday mornings, but he did pitch in and help the pastor with some special projects around the church. He was so good-hearted. I didn't want to disillusion anyone, especially our pastor, about my husband."

"I'd think you would have been desperate for help— and too angry to care what anyone thought of Wayne."

"Being married to an alcoholic is like being married to a child. I could be furious at him, but I was always protective of him. I didn't want other people to think less of him. Looking back, I'm afraid I took my anger out on the kids sometimes, but I didn't see that then. But I was brought up to keep family problems private, and I didn't talk to anyone about Wayne's drinking. As far as being desperate for help, I couldn't see how anyone could do anything. I couldn't ask someone else to get out of bed and drive around in the middle of the night looking for Wayne, just in case he'd passed out on the sidewalk in front of the bar after it closed. I couldn't ask someone else to clean up after him after he'd vomited on the kitchen floor or to pay for the damage he'd done to the neighbor's garden when he drove through it. I saw all those things as our problems—part of the cross we had to bear within the privacy of our own home."

"I'm not suggesting your pastor could have helped you by doing anything like that, but couldn't his counsel have helped you bear your burden?"

"I was tempted a couple of times to ask Pastor Rolf for advice, but we just didn't have that kind of a relationship. And, as I said, I didn't want anyone to know."

I didn't know Vanessa's pastor. Perhaps it's unfair to think that he should have seen the need behind her facade. Perhaps he carried so many burdens for his congregation that he had neither time nor emotional energy to deliberately unearth another. But I pray for a pastor who by his own openness invites my confidence. I want him to ask me how it's going with me and look as if he really cares. If he's there for me, he'll be there for someone like Vanessa.

"What specific steps can the church take to help victims of alcoholism within their congregations?"

- *Education* comes first. If church leaders will take advantage of the information available, they can learn enough about alcoholism and drug abuse to give valuable guidance to families and individuals in their congregations. Their counseling skills will be sharpened as they learn to see the role of alcoholism in the attempted suicide or the divorce or the child abuse case that comes to their attention.

- Pastors, elders, and deacons need to know where *cooperative help* is available. Many churches have members who are recovering alcoholics or have been involved in some area of drug abuse and treatment. These Christians would be blessed to share their experience, strength, and hope with a suffering brother or sister.

- The local church could explore the broader community for *support groups and treatment centers* and invite representatives to speak to their congregations. They could make space available where AA and Al-Anon groups can hold their meetings. They could display literature on drug and alcohol abuse in their libraries and post phone numbers to call for further information.

- *Changed attitudes* come with education and create an atmosphere conducive to helping the victims of alcoholism. The church leadership can set an example of understanding, acceptance, and compassion toward its problem drinkers. They might conduct special prayer vigils for a member who has gone into treatment and give extra support to his family while he is away.

- The pastor of the local church—the shepherd of his flock—should provide *leadership from the pulpit*. Too many preachers would rather avoid the alcohol issue altogether than step on the sensitive toes of either confirmed teetotalers or social drinkers. Anderson Spickard surveyed ministers in his denomination for their views on alcohol abuse. Most believed that the church should do something about the problem, but few had ever preached a sermon on the subject.

I suspect this silence originates at least in part from a desire to avoid identification with strident anti-drinking groups who make smoking and drinking a test of fellowship among Christian believers. Whatever the motivation, the time for silence is past. Ministers must work to find creative and persuasive ways to talk to their congregations about the problem of alcohol abuse and addiction.[10]

A young, dynamic pastor of our church stood before us one morning to declare that he would no longer drink alcoholic beverages. To most of us in the congregation it was an unnecessary vow. Mark's drinking habits had never generated gossip or criticism. If some of us had seen him enjoy a glass of wine at a Rotary Club dinner or a cold beer after a neighborhood ball game, we'd hardly noticed. He was fitting in, after all, with the secular community in which we all lived, and we were rather proud that *our* pastor was such a "regular guy." But Mark had examined his own conscience and decided to take a stand. He was aware of his popularity in the community and his influence on the young people who looked to him for guidance. He had made a personal decision to heed Paul's admonition: "So whether you eat or drink or whatever you do, do it all for the glory of God. Do not cause anyone to stumble" (1 Cor. 10:31–32).

We are called to be salt and light in a needy world, as individual Christians and as church bodies. We need to examine the messages we send by our personal drinking habits and by our attitudes toward those who are victims of a drinking habit that has become addictive. The local church has a unique opportunity to minister to members of its own body and to the surrounding community. Alcoholism is a blight upon our nation. It has crept into the lives of many who look to their church leaders for help and their church families for understanding and support: God equips us for service to our fellow pilgrims when He "comforts us in all our troubles, so that we can comfort those in any trouble with the comfort we ourselves have received from God" (2 Cor. 1:4). If those in the church community will open their minds and hearts to the alcoholics among them, God's people can become part of the solution to a problem that threatens us all.

SUMMARY

- Christians sincerely want to help when they tell us that Christ is the answer to our alcoholism.
- We don't know how to apply Christian slogans to our addiction.
- We need a plan of action.
- We need people who have been there to tell us what to do
- We need the Christian community's cooperation with our secular program.
- AA is not a cult.
- Pastors, priests, and highly moral Christians also fall prey to the disease of alcoholism.
- We need encouragement and understanding from our church families.

"You Have It Licked Now, Don't You?"

Mom, I'm an alcoholic. I'd said the words aloud in the safety of my support group and I'd practiced them over and over in my head, rehearsing for this opportunity to confide in my mother. Now as we settled into a corner booth at Blum's, my heart pounded in anticipation. I would do it now. Before the waitress brought our shrimp sandwiches and mocha shakes, I would tell her. Not too casually. Not too dramatically. I would say it straight on, forcing myself to look into her eyes—those soft brown eyes that had shed so many tears over me.

"Mom, I'm an alcoholic."

"Hush, dear," she said, "Someone might hear you. Of course you're not—you know—an *alcoholic.* You've just been under a lot of strain and gotten into some bad habits. It's that neighborhood you live in and all the cocktail parties. And the children take so much of your energy. I remember what it was like when you children were small. I really think you should hire a cleaning woman. Dad and I would be glad to pay for it. You've just been overtired this past year. Now let's forget all the unpleasantness and put the past behind us where it belongs."

"Mr. Porter, I'm a recovering alcoholic," I said to the school psychologist during a conference about one of our boys. "I haven't been sober very long, and I know the kids have had a hard time." I wanted him to understand what had been going on in our family. My son's behavior was just one more consequence of my disease and my inability to parent effectively.

"Mrs. Johnson, don't put yourself in a category like that. We all have our tendencies to addictions of one kind or another. When I was in college I went through a stage of drinking too much beer. When I found it was interfering with my studying, I cut it out. There's no need for you to call yourself an *alcoholic* when you don't drink anymore. Congratulate yourself that you've been able to learn from past experiences."

"Judy, I'm an alcoholic," I said to a friend.

"Honey," she said, "You're about the furthest thing from an alcoholic I've ever seen. I grew up with a father who was a drunk and I know what an *alcoholic* is! Why, I've known you for a long time and I've never seen you take a drink. If you had a wild time in your younger days, well, who didn't? That's history, honey. Forget it."

"Well, why *can't* you put the past behind you?"

It's important for me to remember where I came from. I'm not living in the past or dwelling on the bad times, but the past is part of who I am today. In order to have an honest relationship with someone, I need to let him know the real me.

I don't always want to do that. Sometimes I want to disown reality. I want to shove those bitter memories out the door of my mind and lock it so they can't get in again. God is so gracious that He doesn't allow me to remember everything at once because that would be overwhelmingly depressing and might send me back to drinking again. His Word promises us forgiveness, but He allows us to live out the consequences of sin. Whether the disease of alcoholism caused the sin or the sin caused the disease, there *was* sin and there *are* consequences.

TAKING THE WRONG ROAD

The biblical meaning of "sin" comes from the Greek *hamartia*, or "missing the mark." That's about the same thing as taking a wrong turn and getting on the wrong road. When an alcoholic drinks, he gets off track. He loses control of his direction. When and if he comes to the dead end of this wrong road, he is lost. In order to find himself, he has to go back to where he took the wrong turn in the first place. However, he can't turn back the calendar. His journey is a mental and emotional one of retracing the steps that led to the dead end. Only when he is back on track can he start over in the right direction.

Now that applies to anyone who is feeling the consequences of sin in his life, but the recovering alcoholic has more steps to retrace than the average person before he finds the right direction. That's because he kept on refusing to see the washouts and chuckholes along the road that had looked so promising in the beginning. He tripped over boulders and fell in the mud and kept on going. He was in denial. When he hit his dead end, he either had to stop or blaze a new trail further into the wilderness. Our hope is that he will face facts and turn around, grope his way back to "square one," and start over. First the wrong road, then the dead end, then the decision. Recovery begins with decision.

"Don't some alcoholics hit one dead end after another?"

Unfortunately too many alcoholics find a way past the first dead end they encounter. They'll climb over every barrier and keep going right up to the edge of the precipice. That's what Wayne did. He hit a dead end when his wife left him. He hit another when he lost his job. Both times he came to Alcoholics Anonymous as a sad and repentant man. But he was unwilling or unable to turn around and go through the necessary steps of recovery. He died from his disease.

> The idea that somehow, someday he will control and enjoy his drinking is the great obsession of every abnormal drinker. The persistence of this illusion is astonishing. Many pursue it into the gates of insanity or death.[1]

There are others of us who come to the dead end and make a decision to turn around but fail to go far enough. We'll either find some side road that looks easier than going back the way we came or we'll return to the same dead end again. Alcoholics have poor memories because they have damaged their brains with alcohol. Obsession overpowers reason.

When I first came to the dead end of my particular road, I was sure I'd never drink again. My failing marriage began to heal. My self-respect began to reappear. But the months and years of anesthetizing myself had left me numb. As the numbness lifted and feeling returned, I began to hurt. I felt the pain of remorse. Forgotten incidents replayed themselves in my mind and tortured me in the still hours of the night. Life was hard. Then my addiction cried out to be fed and I began to rationalize and justify having another drink.

Just one, to take the edge off. Just one, to feel normal again. Why had I been so quick to decide that I was an alcoholic? My mother was probably right. There had been too many cocktail parties over the holiday season. Now that my pattern of daily drinking had been broken, now that I understood the pitfalls, I could control my drinking. I told myself these lies until my resistance weakened and died. My great obsession was the victor. I'd take that one drink, knowing that I was lying to myself, knowing that one would not be enough, just as it had never been enough.

FROM OBSESSION TO COMPULSION

An amazing thing happens when an alcoholic takes a drink after a period of sobriety. Obsession becomes compulsion. Look at the definitions of these two words.

> **Obsession**: Compulsive *preoccupation* with a fixed idea or unwanted feeling. **Compulsion**: 1. The act of compelling or forcing. 2. The state of being compelled. 3. An *irresistible* impulse to act.[2]

I've emphasized the key words in those definitions. If you've never had such an experience, maybe I can explain it this way:

It's something like when you go into labor with your second (or third or fourth) baby. You forget this part while you're knitting booties and repainting the nursery. You go through nine months of excited anticipation. You can't wait for that first sign of labor. But then the pain begins. Suddenly you remember what the last time was like and you want out. There's no turning back. The only way out is through the midst of the pain.

Of course there's a difference in an alcoholic binge and childbirth. The outcome of labor is joy. The outcome of the drinking episode is disaster.

The condition of my marriage was downgraded from serious to critical. My self-respect fell through the cracks of my broken promises. I was on my way down the dark and familiar road that would lead to another dead end. I kept turning around and starting in the right direction, only to fail and turn back. And each time I would forget what it was like to surrender my soul to alcohol. Each slip began with an obsession that became a compulsion that enslaved me until I cried out for help once more.

"You eventually learned from experience, didn't you?"

Most alcoholics are incapable of learning from experience. I was. But I began to trust the experiences of others. Finally I was beaten down enough to take directions from the people who were trying to help me. They'd taken the same wrong turn, hit the same dead end, and found the way back again.

These people told me I would have to do something that I wasn't good at doing—face reality. "Give up," they said. "You've lost the battle." I had to see that I was defeated and completely incapable of helping myself. My recovery began with surrender. The men who started AA knew that was where recovery began when they wrote their First Step:

We admitted we were powerless over alcohol—that our lives had become unmanageable.

I'd heard that step before. My recovering alcoholic friends told me from the beginning that an admission of powerlessness was an absolute prerequisite for successful sobriety. But I'd thought maybe I was different. I'd had to prove to myself that I'd lost all control over my drinking. It didn't take me long.

Well, now what? I thought. *If I'm powerless, where's the hope?* "Trust us," my friends said. "Take one step at a time." So I laid down my shield of pride and planted my feet firmly on that first step. But then . . .

- I went to a New Year's Eve party and had a terrible time. We played charades and I was so self-conscious I wanted to crawl under the rug. I knew nothing would ever be fun again.
- I went to a movie and the theater audience roared with laughter over the lovable drunk. I sat like an unlovable stone.
- I read an article that said alcoholism is definitely *not* a disease.
- A former friend snubbed me at the grocery store, and I wondered what I'd done that I didn't remember.
- I remembered.

I didn't know how to be sober. I hated my sour personality, but there was no merriment in my heart. I couldn't sleep nights because of the guilt that stabbed at me. I was ill at ease around people, and I was afraid to be alone. I exhausted myself with crying. I thought I would probably go insane.

"Didn't you know you needed God?"

I should have known. I'd been crying out to Him for so long, but I needed to be still and know that He was there. I'd put my trust in the people who were giving me directions, but some of them, I found, had feet of clay. Soft-spoken Ed turned out to be an ex-convict; my kind sponsor, Ruth, had left her husband and was living with another man; old "keep-the-plug-in-the-jug" Karl was drinking again. *This is successful sober living?* I asked myself. They said things like:

- "Judge not."
- "Stick with the winners."
- "Put principles before personalities."
- "It's time for another step."

I'd been so busy letting go of my pride and my authority over my life that I'd forgotten to look for a replacement to take charge of me. My fellow recovering alcoholics didn't want that job. They were just there to give me directions and support me as I tried to follow them. I looked at the Second Step.

[We] came to believe that a Power greater than ourselves could restore us to sanity.

Would you believe it? Years and years before, the men and women who were struggling to stay sober felt just like I did—that they were losing their minds. They'd written a Step telling how they'd worked it out. They'd found a Power greater than themselves.

I believed in God. I believed He'd answered my prayers for help and brought me to this program. But a *personal* God who would restore me to sanity when He knew I'd brought this confusion on myself? Wasn't I supposed to buck up and shoulder some responsibility now that I was thinking straight?

"Don't kid yourself," my mentors said. "You're not thinking straight yet. You've killed off a lot of brain cells over the years, and there's a large hunk of your brain that's damaged. Maybe you'll never be able to think straight again."

"Stop!" I said. "How can you tell me a Power greater than myself can restore me to sanity if my brain is damaged?"

"Didn't the blind man see again?" someone asked.

"Well, I'm not all that crazy," declared my Pride. "Surely there's something I can do."

"There is," said my sponsor. "Take the Third Step."

[We] made a decision to turn our will and our lives over to the care of God *as we understood Him.*

That called for the final abandonment of ego and self-will. I had admitted my powerlessness, faced the mess I'd made of things, and become aware of my insanity. Now I was supposed to give up completely on myself and my own resources, and turn everything over to a God I hardly knew. Later, when I came to know Him more intimately, I found this passage of Scripture:

Humble yourselves, therefore, under God's mighty hand, that he may lift you up in due time. Cast all your anxiety on him because he cares for you. Be self-controlled and alert. Your enemy the devil prowls

around like a roaring lion looking for someone to
devour.

(l Peter 5:6–8)

My anonymous friends had the right idea, and they
had things in the right order. I *could* be restored to sanity
(self-controlled and alert), but only after I'd turned my will
and my life over to His care (cast all my anxiety on Him).

"Is the alcoholic's brain really damaged?"

Because of the *abnormal* way the alcoholic metabo-
lizes or processes alcohol, drinking causes a permanent
chemical change in his brain cells. These changes will
continue to affect him in the beginning stages of his
recovery.

Terence T. Gorski and Merlene Miller, specialists in
relapse prevention, have written about the syndrome they
call Post Acute Withdrawal (PAW). The following symptoms have been identified as contributing to this syndrome:

- the inability to think clearly or concentrate for
  more than a few minutes,
- impairment of abstract reasoning,
- difficulty in remembering,
- mood swings from emotional overreactions to
  numbness or lack of feeling,
- disturbance of normal sleep patterns,
- physical coordination problems,
- low tolerance to stressful situations.[3]

Some or all of these symptoms may begin to appear a
week or two after abstinence from alcohol begins. God
gives us a little grace period while we go through the *acute*

withdrawal! That's what we call detoxification. But getting the poison out of our systems is only one tiny step toward sobriety. Then because of the physiological changes that have taken place in our bodies and because of the psychological stress of trying to live *sober* with the pain of reality, we forget the appointment, trip over the dog, or read the same simple paragraph over and over without comprehension. We were in better shape when we were drinking, we think. We suspect we are going crazy.

The founders of AA, one of them a medical doctor, observed the varying degrees of physical, mental, and emotional symptoms in newly sober alcoholics and designed a program to deal with them all. When AA said alcoholics needed to be "restored to sanity," they meant exactly that.

When most people think about alcoholism they think only of the alcohol-based symptoms and forget about the sobriety-based symptoms. Yet it is the sobriety-based symptoms, especially Post Acute Withdrawal, that make sobriety so difficult.

The presence of brain dysfunction has been documented in 75–95% of recovering alcoholics tested. Recent research indicates that the symptoms of long-term withdrawal associated with alcohol and drug-related damage to the brain may contribute to many cases of relapse.

Recovery causes a great deal of stress. Many chemically dependent people never learn to manage stress without alcohol and drug use. The stress aggravates the brain dysfunction and makes the symptoms worse. The severity of PAW depends upon two things: the severity of the brain dysfunction caused by the addiction and the amount of psycho-social stress experienced in recovery.[4]

The good news is that the brain and the nervous system have marvelous powers of recuperation and the damage is usually reversible with proper treatment and continuous sobriety. What a joy it is when we can face the day with its inevitable stress and know that we can cope without a pain-dulling anesthetic. Our abilities to think, remember, and concentrate return; our emotions stabilize; we can sleep at night and stay awake in the daytime; and—wonder of wonders—we really *can* cope!

WHEN IT'S TOO LATE

Sometimes, if the alcoholic continues to drink into the final stages of his addiction, there is permanent brain damage.

Years of heavy drinking have depleted his supply of thiamine, a vitamin necessary for growth and mainte-nance of nerve tissue, and his brain becomes diseased and shrinks in size. Two of the most common forms of alcohol related brain disease are *Wernicke's syn-drome* and *Korsakoff's psychosis*. Wernicke's syn-drome is often reversible by injections of thiamine. Korsakoff's psychosis is an irreversible brain disease that puts the alcoholic on skid row or in a nursing home.[5]

The cold facts show that most alcoholics who con-tinue to drink die before they reach that stage of their disease. They die of delirium tremens, cirrhosis, heart attack, or stroke; they die intentionally by suicide or accidentally in drownings, fires, and automobiles.

Those of us who have been blessed with sobriety are only alive and sane by the grace of God.

A NEW BEGINNING

I had faced the truth about my life and my disease, I had listened to the advice of others who were getting well, and I had put it all in God's hands. Every morning I said, "Thank you, God, for my sobriety. Please help me stay away from the first drink today." My physical compulsion to drink faded with time; my mental obsession was apt to reappear with every bump in the road of painful reality. I trusted God to restore me to sanity, but I wanted Him to do it faster.

For years I had been solving problems with alcohol. I didn't know how to cope with normal stress, let alone the mental and physical stress that accompanies the beginning stages of recovery from addiction. Normally, my coping skills would have been sharpened with experience as I grew in maturity. But at thirty-two, I was far from mature. I'd learned to buffer every painful experience with my chosen anesthetic.

Like other recovering alcoholics, I found myself in a grown-up world with adolescent emotions. A mountain of problems had accumulated in the last years of my drinking, and my resources for dealing with them were pitifully inadequate. In order to develop effective ways of coping with present reality, it was necessary for me to look at the painful past and understand where I'd gotten off the track.

LOOKING BACK

As a very young woman I watched my four-year-old son die from an injection that was intended to cure him from a minor illness. I could not face the agonizing reality of his death. I declined the doctor's offer of sleeping pills; I fought sleep, dreading the renewed onslaught of pain that would come with every reawakening. Instead of a pill, I accepted the highball a sympathetic neighbor placed in my hand and found relief in the numbness the alcohol brought. My habitual drinking began on that terrible day. In those days one drink was enough, and that was my daily ration. Getting high was for celebration, I thought, not for mourning.

Because of my physiological and psychological makeup, I was programmed for addiction. The circumstances served as a *trigger*. At some time in the months or years that followed, I crossed the line into addiction. I went from *choosing* to drink to *having* to drink. One was no longer enough, ever. The progression was slow and insidious. It was eight years before I admitted to myself that there might be a problem with my drinking and another year of frantic denial before I sought help.

I write about my personal tragedy because it is part of my past and was a foundation upon which to build my alcoholism. Many people have faced tragic loss without turning to alcohol. Others have welcomed the temporary effects of liquor or prescription drugs without becoming addicted. My young husband grieved in his own way, sleeping or retreating into silence when he wasn't finding solace in his work. Grief was the catalyst for my alcoholism, but it might have been something else that year or the next. I was predisposed to my disease.

In escaping from my pain I managed to avoid confrontation with lesser problems. Turning away from conflict was easier than dealing with the inevitable dissention that is part of any close relationship. My marriage suffered the most. Years of alcoholic drinking had taken their toll and left the relationship between my husband and me in critical condition. My parenting, too, was inconsistent and inadequate. Our four children needed the security and stability of a mature and sober mother.

There was no denying that my life had become unmanageable. For too long I had sidestepped my responsibilities as a wife and mother. But sobriety demanded change. It was time to face my world and its difficulties head on, with courage and a clear mind.

LOOKING WITHIN

If I hadn't put God in charge by making a decision to turn my will and my life over to His care, I would have been utterly discouraged. It was time to let Him lead me as I began to pick up the broken pieces of my life. I began this process by following directions and taking AA's Fourth Step.

[We] made a searching and fearless moral inventory of ourselves.

With God's help I turned my attention inward and took stock of what was there. A major cleaning job was in order. I needed to weed out destructive traits and coax other traits into maturity. There were seeds of promise among the weeds, and my friends told me to look at those, too.

It has been said that the alcoholic's problem is not alcohol, it is self-will. We want what we want when we want it. It was hard to look at that kind of selfishness in myself, but it was there. I saw that my self-will was a breeding ground for resentment, intolerance, anger, fear, and insecurity. I recognized those things and more as I proceeded with my inventory.

Father Bill, a Catholic priest and an alcoholic, says that the Fourth Step is the spiritual crux of the AA program. Step Four takes us into the garbage of our souls, he says, and it is among the garbage that we find God. I understand his meaning. It was in taking an honest look at myself that I realized my own helplessness and the absolute necessity for God in my life. He alone could help me bear the truth. He alone could grant the courage to "change the things I could." My new way of life demanded that I be fearless. When humiliating memories pounded at the door of my mind and threatened my fragile serenity, I began to let them in.

My fellow alcoholics told me that I must share my inventory with someone else. They pointed me to the Fifth Step—a growth step for me because it called for a further shrinking of my pride.

[We] admitted to God, to ourselves, and to another human being the exact nature of our wrongs.

AA recommends taking this step with a minister or priest. Having no church connection, I chose another recovering alcoholic and poured out my life to her. She patiently listened to all the sins of commission and omission that I had dredged up in my inventory and then helped me search for more. She shared with me her own past failures, her present successes, and her future hope. She helped me to look at my unhealthy attachment to some of my destructive character traits. In her unconditional acceptance of the real me, she was a channel for God's love and forgiveness.

I was both dismayed and relieved to see my inner self laid bare. I'd known there was ugliness and deformity beneath the mask I'd been wearing for so long. The image I'd tried to project to others reeked of hypocrisy and had to be discarded with the rest of the garbage. My mandatory soul-searching had uncovered the dirt and debris beneath my facade, and the revelation appalled me. Yet, there was hope in a new awareness of God's grace. As Father Bill said, I'd found "God among the garbage."

Jesus understood our sinful hearts when he said:

> What comes out of a man is what makes him "unclean." For from within, out of men's hearts, come evil thoughts, sexual immorality, theft, murder, adultery, greed, malice, deceit, lewdness, envy, slander, arrogance and folly. All these evils come from inside and make a man "unclean."
>
> *(Mark 7:20–23)*

I was determined to be rid of whatever evils lurked in my heart and eager to start the weeding process. I wanted to be clean and freed from the guilt that might cause me to drink again. My desire was a fulfillment of the Sixth Step:

[We] were entirely ready to have God remove all these defects of character.

With my new awareness of God as Someone who knew and understood my sinful soul, prayer came more easily. I could feel His work in my life as one sober day followed another. I had cried, "Help, God!" and He had answered. He was really there! I believed He would answer as I followed the Seventh Step:

[We] humbly asked Him to remove our shortcomings.

Something went wrong at this stage of my recovery. God was slow in removing my shortcomings and my defects of character. They showed up most clearly in the area of my relationships with others—my husband, my children, my parents, my friends. When I ran to my support group with tales of unfair criticism or lack of appreciation, they said I was harboring resentment and self-pity. When I became defensive, they pointed to my pride. "Move on," they said. "You've come to the Eighth and Ninth Steps":

[We] made a list of all people we had harmed, and became willing to make amends to them all. And [We] made direct amends to such people wherever possible, except when to do so would injure them or others.

Wasn't I trying? I protested. But it was too hard and too slow. They told me to try harder, that it would take the rest of my life.

No one seemed to understand what I was going through. Maybe God understood, but where *was* He anyway? Some days I wondered if He'd taken a leave of absence from His position as Director of my life. I felt alone as I tried to weed out the flaws and make the amends. As I worked on one glaring fault, another would spring up beside it. As I tried to make amends to one person, I seemed to be stepping on someone else's toes. I was in worse shape than I'd thought. I'd bared my soul, thrown away my mask, and counted on God to take away the garbage. Instead, He seemed to have left me to fend for myself. The euphoria I'd felt in the beginning weeks of sobriety faded into discouragement. My burden of guilt grew heavier. I drank again.

"Didn't you know Christ died for that guilt?"

I'd gone to Sunday School as a child, I'd memorized the Twenty-third Psalm to earn a Bible, but the gospel message had failed to penetrate my heart. Now as I plodded along my personal road to recovery from alcoholism, falling into periodic relapse, I was coming to see God in a new way. I was the prodigal daughter on my way home. Although I seemed to have found God in the humbling first steps of sobriety, the solid, abiding faith of the Christian eluded me for many years. I believe each of us comes to the Cross in our own way—or in His way for us—and for me it was the path of repeated failure and overwhelming guilt.

I wore my sobriety like a body cast over broken bones. After each alcoholic slip, I would shoulder my ever-increasing load of guilt and reach out for God's forgiveness and guidance again. Each relapse added to the garbage heap. My marriage died. Guilt flourished.

REDEMPTION

"All I want is a clean slate," I said to my counselor as I embarked upon a second marriage.

"You have it," he assured me. But somehow I knew it wasn't his to give.

I sensed that there was a price to be paid. I would pay the price, I decided, by accepting the guilt without complaint. I would not run from the pain that I deserved. I would stay sober. This time I would nurture my marriage and the five motherless children that my new husband brought to our union. I would redeem myself in the eyes of God and the world by devoting myself to the care and feeding of our newly blended family.

It may be more obvious to the reader than it was to me that I had returned to my executive position as director of my life. My unmanageable life had become manageable, I thought. "You're doing such a good job," people said. "You can put the past behind you now." I basked in the warm praise of old friends and family members who encouraged me. In their eyes I had recovered from whatever it was that caused my excessive drinking. Most of the time I thought of myself as they did—*recovered* instead of *recovering*. I had a fresh start in life and a program to follow—if I should need it.

I gave God a share of the credit for my increasing periods of sobriety, but I congratulated myself for developing a measure of self-discipline and will-power. Communication with my Higher Power dropped low on my priority list during these intervals of complacency.

With the challenge of a new marriage and the mothering of nine youngsters as they grew from pre-adolescence to young adulthood, it was God's miracle that I stayed sober at all, but I did—ninety-nine percent of the time. I think now that God allowed those long sober periods in order that our transplanted children could take root and grow in a relatively stable atmosphere.

I suspect He also allowed the dark periods when I would stumble over my own self-sufficiency in order to draw me closer to Him. He let me slip into my old ways of pride and resentment and self-pity. (Do you know what a martyr a mother of nine can be?) He let the obsession build until I drank again. Then He led me back to the program of Alcoholics Anonymous and its tools.

"Did you think you'd graduated?" my new support group asked. "You haven't finished the course yet. Go back and review the steps from the beginning, and then look at the Tenth Step":

[We] continued to take personal inventory and when we were wrong promptly admitted it.

I knew it all, and that made it harder. I knew—but I'd forgotten—that I was powerless over alcohol. My old life had been unmanageable, but hadn't I been doing pretty well with this one? "Take a look," my friends said. "That's what the inventory is for."

So I delved once more into the hidden parts of my inner self. One look and I cried out for God to come and be my guide as I waded through the debris. There behind the walls of pride and complacency was a lot of junk I thought I'd gotten rid of in my first inventory. Beside it a whole new heap of garbage had accumulated. I planted new seedlings of humility where tender shoots had shriveled and died for lack of light.

And when we were wrong, we promptly admitted it, the Tenth Step said. I had been wrong to think I could manage my own life without God's help. I'd thrown away one mask and created another. Again, I was relieved and appalled at what lay beneath my facade of self-sacrificing wife and mother, producer of creative casseroles and home-baked bread, keeper of the peace, and laundress extraordinaire. There was a terrible sense of discouragement in seeing my lack of progress during my "mostly sober" years. I'd asked God to remove my defects of character, but they were still there. My burden of guilt grew heavier. In despair, I turned to God in a new way. AA's Eleventh Step was there to guide me:

[We] sought through prayer and meditation to improve our conscious contact with God as we understood Him, praying only for knowledge of His will for us and the power to carry it out.

I had made contact with God, or He with me, in my days of desperation, but then I'd left Him behind and gone my own way. No wonder all the garbage was still there. I had no power of my own to change myself. I had to rely on God to give me the power. That was the answer: I needed power!

"Wait," said my friends. "Begin at the beginning of the step."

- Seek through prayer and meditation to improve your conscious contact with God.
- Pray for His will for you.

Those things would have to come before the power.

UP THE DOWN ESCALATOR

I've tried to give you a picture of the recovery process for me. Perhaps you can guess where my road was leading me. The process is not the same for everyone, nor is the culmination. For me the process has been painfully slow, but the climax was Jesus. I came to know Christ as I sought a closer contact with God. Christ *is* our contact with God. He comes to us now in the person of the Holy Spirit. It is in the Spirit that we find the power.

Consider the first part of the Twelfth Step in the Alcoholics Anonymous program:

Having had a spiritual awakening as the result of these steps ...

The men who founded AA were Christians. They searched God's Word for the keys to a spiritual awakening, for they'd found that their only defense against alcoholism was a spiritual one. Dr. Samuel Shoemaker, an Episcopal clergyman, and Father Ed Dowling of the Jesuit order heartily endorsed the program of Alcoholics Anonymous in its pioneering stages and were treasured friends and advisors to the organization from its birth in 1935.

Father Dowling was the first clergyman of his faith to note the surprising resemblance between the

spiritual Exercises of St. Ignatius (founder of the
Jesuit order) and the Twelve Steps of Alcoholics
Anonymous. As a result, he was quick to write in 1940
the first Catholic recommendation of A.A. of which
we have any knowledge.[6]

The founders of AA were not called to lead suffering
alcoholics to Christ but to lead them to restored health and
a spiritual awakening. Christian missionaries to Third
World countries know that starving people can better hear
the gospel after their stomachs have been filled. So too, the
early missionaries to alcoholics found that sobriety and a
spiritual awakening had to precede a heart-knowledge of
God's provision for our salvation through Christ. These
pioneers had to be God-inspired to innovate a simple
program that would be so effective in helping the formerly
hopeless alcoholic. For the past fifty-six years, hundreds of
thousands of men and women have found life-changing
power in the steps of Alcoholics Anonymous. Because it is
an anonymous program with no formal structure or
membership list, exact statistics are unavailable, but the
angels surely sing over every life restored to sobriety and
sanity.

LIGHTING THE WAY

In 1960, as a newly recovering alcoholic, I attended
an International Convention to celebrate the Twenty-fifth
Anniversary of Alcoholics Anonymous. Sober alcoholics
from all over the world sat shoulder to shoulder, packed
into a huge Southern California stadium, as we listened to
the inspiring testimonies of Bill W., AA's co-founder, and
many others—doctors, actors, statesmen, and corporation
presidents. At one moment in the evening program, the

lights were turned out and each of us lit a single match. Thousands of tiny flames lit the darkness and blended into a glow of such radiance it made my heart turn over. There was a breathless silence as we each felt the impact of the moment. We were lighting the way for one another as we celebrated our miraculous rescue from a world of darkness. Each of us represented at least three others whose worlds had been darkened because of our addiction. The program of Alcoholics Anonymous had been God's instrument for our changed lives. My heart sang with praise for Him.

OTHER ROADS

There are other roads to sobriety besides the two-lane highway where God and the fellowship of AA work side by side. Perhaps you know a perfectly wonderful person who has been sober in AA for many years without acknowledging God. Or maybe your friend Bob Wilson, who used to drink like a fish, just "up and quit" one day without any help from anyone. Then there's your cousin Hazel, who was delivered from her bondage to alcohol during a revival meeting and has been living like a saint ever since. And everyone knows about Dick Smith, church member and practicing alcoholic, who insists AA didn't "work" for him. All of these examples are exceptions to the rule that recovery from alcoholism requires a commitment to God plus a new way of life.

Recovery rarely takes a straight path for any of us. Even after twenty years of continual sobriety, recovery for me is still a process, not an accomplished fact. We are each sober one day at a time and by the grace of God, whether or not we recognize that grace.

Sobriety for an alcoholic is a miracle, however God

chooses to work it out for each individual. But sobriety is not an end in itself, and most of us have a lot of catching up to do. We need to learn a new way of life in order to remain sober and grow spiritually. That's what AA's Twelve Steps are all about. I believe that the process outlined in the steps is necessary for every recovering alcoholic. If Hazel's miracle was an instantaneous, straight-path, permanent recovery, God sped up the process for His purposes.

Dick Smith may have a problem committing himself to AA's way of life because of his interpretation of one of my favorite biblical passages:

> Three times I pleaded with the Lord to take it away from me. But he said to me, "My grace is sufficient for you, for my power is made perfect in weakness."
> (2 Cor. 12:8–9)

I agree with Dick that God's grace is sufficient in every circumstance. But perhaps he feels that Bible study, prayer meetings, and faithful attendance at worship services ought to give him what he needs to overcome his drinking problem. Maybe he feels somewhat guilty in turning for help to a spiritual program outside his church. He waits for a direct God-to-Dick miracle, when God could bless him with healing through other *people*. We are here for him. Helping Dick is part of our own healing, a crucial element of the Twelfth Step:

Having had a spiritual awakening as the result of those steps, we tried to carry this message to alcoholics and to practice these principles in all our affairs.

Every recovering alcoholic walks his own road to healing. Our spiritual growth undergirds stable sobriety, and each of us experiences that growth in a different way.

Some of us are Christians to begin with or find Christ
along our own Damascus road. Some of us fail to
acknowledge the Source of our healing, crediting instead
our own will power and self-discipline. Others give credit
to a program or a treatment center or a nonspecific Higher
Power. It is all a miracle by the grace of God.

With a little prodding from God's ambassadors, one of
whom was a recovering alcoholic, I found myself at a local
Bible study for women. On the first day, leafing through
the unfamiliar Bible, I came upon this passage of Scripture:

> The Spirit helps us in our weakness. We do not know
> what we ought to pray for, but the Spirit himself
> intercedes for us with groans that words cannot
> express.
>
> (Rom. 8:26)

Those words had a profound effect upon me. It was as
if someone had pointed to a map and said, "See, this is
where you started and this is how far you've come." The
Spirit helped me in my weakness on that day when I began
my spiritual journey. I didn't know how to pray as I had no
words to express the depth of my despair. I wasn't even
sure anyone was listening. The Spirit interceded and
brought me down this long road to meet my Redeemer.

The road goes on, paved with God's grace, as I pursue
the design for living that AA has given me in its program.
I've taken the Steps to a place of stability and serenity.
I have a daily reprieve from the bondage of addiction if I
follow the guidelines of those who have gone before me. I
pray the same reprieve for you and your loved one. I pray
you a miracle.

SUMMARY

- We need you to believe us when we tell you we are alcoholics.
- When we come to a dead end in our drinking, we either turn around and begin to get well or ignore the warning and blaze a trail further into the wilderness.
- Our recoveries begin with admission of our own helplessness.
- We need to trust God to take over.
- Alcohol has taken its toll with us and recovery is *hard*.
- Sometimes we make false starts and take detours on our way to recovery.
- When our obsession becomes a compulsion, we lose our choice about drinking.
- AA's Twelve Steps are designed for our healing.
- We are sober by the grace of God.

Notes

CHAPTER ONE: "Is It Really a Disease?"

[1]American Medical Association: *Manual on Alcoholism* (Chicago: AMA, 1968), 6.

[2]"About Alcholism," *Grapevine* (November 1975), 44.

[3]Janice Keller Phelps, M.D.; Alan E. Nourse, M.D., *The Hidden Addiction and How to Get Free* (Boston: Little, Brown & Co., 1986), 87.

[4]Ibid., 232.

[5]Ibid., 27.

[6]V. E. Davis, et. al., "Alcohol, Amines, and Alkalolids; A Possible Biochemical Basis for Alcohol Addiction," *Science* 167 (1970): 1005–7.

[7]David L. Ohlms, M.D., *The Disease of Alcoholism* (Belleville, Ill.: Gary Whiteaker Corporation, 1988) 14–17.

[8]Terence T. Gorski; Merlene Miller, *Staying Sober: A Guide for Relapse Prevention* (Independence, Mo.: Independence Press, 1986), 40.

[9]Terence Monmaney; Karen Springen; Mary Hager, "Alcohol and the Family," *Newsweek* (18 January 1988), 66.

[10]Daniel Goleman, "Drug Addiction Linked to Brain Irregularities," *Santa Barbara News Press* (7 July, 1990), A15.

[11]Ibid.

[12]Phelps and Nourse, *The Hidden Addiction*, 35–36.

[13]Roland E. Herrington, M.D.; George R. Jacobson, Ph.D.; David G. Benzer, D.O., *Alcohol and Drug Abuse Handbook* (St. Louis: Warren H. Green, Inc., 1987), 183.

[14]Ibid., 190.

[15]Ibid., 192.

CHAPTER TWO: "Why Do You Want to Die?"

[1]Lewis J. Lord, "Coming to Grips With Alcoholism," *U.S. News and World Report* (30 November 1987), 56.

[2]Herrington and Benzer, *Alcohol and Drug Abuse Handbook*, 220.

[3]Larry L. King, "Sixty," *Parade Magazine* (5 November 1989), 8.

[4]Anonymous, "Diary of a Drunk," *Time* (30 November 1987), 84.

[5]Barnaby Conrad, *Time is All We Have* (New York: Dell Publishing, 1986), 199.

CHAPTER THREE: "Where Did We Go Wrong?"

[1]Sharon Wegscheider, *Another Chance: Hope and Health for the Alcoholic Family* (Palo Alto: Science and Behavior Books, Inc., 1981), 33.

[2]Lewis Lord, "Coming to Grips With Alcoholism," 56.

[3]"To the Mother and Father of an Alcoholic," (New York: Al-Anon Family Group Headquarters, Inc., 1971), 5.

[4]Barbra Minar, "Parents in Crisis—Parents in Pain" (Pamphlet, privately printed).

[5]Ibid.

CHAPTER FIVE: "Is Daddy Home Yet?"

[1]Anderson Spickard, M.D.; Barbara R. Thompson, *Dying For a Drink: What You Should Know About Alcoholism* (Waco, Texas: Word Books, 1985), 79.

[2]Wegscheider, *Another Chance*, 85.

[3]Monmaney, Springen, and Hager, "Alcohol and the Family," 62.

[4]Ibid., 64.

[5]Ibid., 63.

[6]Bonnie Johnson, "Breaking the Bond of Silence," *People* (18 April 1988), 108.

CHAPTER SIX: "Where Do We Turn for Help?"

[1]"Detachment," (New York: Al-Anon Family Group Headquarters, Inc., 1981).

[2]*Alcoholics Anonymous* (New York: Alcoholics Anonymous Publishing, Inc., 1955), 59–60.

[3]Frank Minirth; Paul Meier; Siegfried Fink; Walter Byrd; Don Hawkins, *Taking Control: New Hope for Substance Abusers and Their Families* (Grand Rapids: Baker Book House, 1988), 79.

[4]Ibid., 80.

[5]Spickard and Thompson, *Dying for a Drink*, 182–3.

CHAPTER SEVEN: "How Can We Help?"

[1]Clinton White, *Wise Up! How?* (Plainfield, N.J.: Logos International, 1970), 16.

[2]Spickard and Thompson, *Dying for a Drink*, 127.

[3]Alexander C. DeJong, *Help and Hope for the Alcoholic*, (Wheaton, Ill.: Tyndale House Publishers, Inc., 1982), 18.

[4]Ibid., 20.

[5]Minirth, Meier, Fink, Byrd, and Hawkins, *Taking Control*, 20.

[6]William Lenters, *The Freedom We Crave: Addiction: The Human Condition* (Grand Rapids: William B. Eerdmans Publishing Co., 1985), 80.

[7]Jamie Buckingham, "Confessions of a Sipping Saint," *Charisma & Christian Life* (March 1989), 64.

[8]Virginia Culver, *The Denver Post* (29 June 1984), 15C.

[9]Walter A. Kortrey, "Our Drinking Dilemma," *The Lutheran* (17 November 1982), 5.

[10]Spickard and Thompson, *Dying for a Drink*, 185.

CHAPTER EIGHT: "You Have It Licked Now, Don't You?"

[1]*Alcoholics Anonymous* (New York: Alcoholics Anonymous Publishing, Inc., 1955), 30.

[2]*American Heritage Dictionary* (Boston: Houghton Mifflin Company, 1982), pp. 304, 858.

[3]Gorski and Miller, *Staying Sober*, 59.

[4]Ibid., 57–58.

[5]Spickard and Thompson, *Dying for a Drink*, 49.

[6]*Alcoholics Anonymous Comes of Age: A Brief History of A.A.* (New York: Alcoholics Anonymous World Services, Inc., 1957), 253–254.

Resources For Further Information

Al-Anon Family Group Headquarters, Inc.
  P.O. Box 862
  Midtown Station
  New York, N.Y. 10018–0862
  800-344-2666 (includes Alaska, Hawaii, Puerto Rico, and
    Virgin Islands)

The National Association for Children of Alcoholics
  Suite 201
  31706 Coast Highway
  South Laguna, CA 92677

National Council on Alcoholism
  12 W. 21st Street
  New York, NY 10010
  800-NCA-CALL

National Clearinghouse for Alcohol and
    Drug Abuse Information
  P.O. Box 2345
  Rockville, MD 20852
  301-468-2600

Alcoholics Anonymous
  P.O. Box 459
  Grand Central Station
  New York, NY 10017

Overcomers Outreach, Inc.
 2290 W. Whittier Blvd., Suite D
 La Habra, CA 90631
 213-697-3994

Substance Abusers Victorious
 One Cascade Plaza, Suite 1222
 Akron, OH 44308
 216-253-5444